FLYING
WITH
WHITE EAGLE

pioneer homesteader

&

bush pilot

Ayliffe "Pat" Carey

1903-1999

In his own words –
as told to
Ben Nuttall-Smith

FLYING WITH WHITE EAGLE

2nd Edition

copyright © Ben Nuttall-Smith 2016

Author: Ben Nuttall-Smith
Publisher: Rutherford Press
             www.rutherfordpress.ca

For information, contact:
Rutherford Press,
Richmond, BC, Canada
info@rutherfordpress.ca
www.rutherfordpress.ca
Printed in the United States of America and Canada

ISBN (paperback) # 978-0-9951743-2-0
ISBN (ebook)   # 978-0-9951743-3-7

1st edition printed – July 2014
2nd edition printed – September 2016

www.bennuttal-smith.ca

to Margot

best friend, partner, travel companion

and primary editor

cover art and pencil sketches

Ben Nuttall-Smith 2014

CONTENTS

PART ONE – FRASER VALLEY PIONEER

PART TWO – FLYING WITH EAGLES

PART THREE – LUCK RUNS OUT

FORWARD

In early 1996, as a volunteer for the *Sunshine Coast White Cane Society*, I met Ayliffe "Pat" Carey, a blind ex-bush pilot. When he heard I wrote stories for the local newspaper, Pat asked me if I'd consent to write his biography. I soon began weekly visits to the Carey trailer home where Pat and his wife Jean told me exciting and often humorous stories of his life from Fraser Valley pioneer to bush pilot.

Pat's earlier experiences as a young man growing up in British Columbia's Fraser Valley and as homesteader and logger, provide an exceptional insight into pioneering days in the first decades of the twentieth Century. His stories of flying from Chilliwack, B.C. to Canada's Far North are fascinating tales of aviation history.

―――――――

Pat tells his story as if he's reliving every moment. His attention to detail and his memory for names are amazing.

―――――――

Pat Carey died on October 9th, 1999, aged 96. Following his memorial service, Pat's widow Jean asked me to honour the memory of her late husband by continuing the biological work.

―――――――

Remarks and explanations in italics are those of the author and do not represent the words of Ayliffe Pat Carey.

PART ONE

FRASER VALLEY PIONEER

FAMILY ROOTS

My Grandmother Jackson was a very strong-willed person with a mind of her own. The only daughter of a wealthy family with a large estate in the middle of Scotland, Grandma fell in love with William Ayliffe Carey, the eldest son of the head gardener. The Jacksons would have nothing to do with the thought of their Clara marrying a "commoner", so the two lovers eloped south to Glen Gables where they were married at *The Blacksmith Shop*, a place where nuptials could be discreetly and inexpensively arranged.

When the young couple moved further south to Bristol, thanks to his previous experience working with horses on the estate, Grandfather William was able to get a job driving a horse-drawn trolley. The trolley ran on tracks through the main area of the town. Grandfather continued at that job until Sir Walter White, owner of the trolley service, decided to electrify the system. Grandpa immediately resolved to study electricity and soon became a driver on one of the new tramcars. He would remain at that position until 1910, when he decided to join my father's family in Canada.

My dad, William Thomas Ayliffe, was the eldest of the new Carey clan, followed in close order by Vivian, Cecil and Daisy. When Father finished school, he joined the Royal Marines and was sent to China and then to India. During his seven years of military service, he formed a close friendship with a Colonel Coote.

Both men probably finished their tour of duty at about the same time and returned to England together. Colonel Coote decided to travel to Canada to explore the new country he'd heard so much about.

After a few years, Colonel Coote returned to Bristol and renewed his friendship with my dad. At that time, jobs in England were scarce. Father had found employment as a postman in Chipping-Sodbury, on the outskirts of Bristol. He married Nelly Ellen Dolly Jeffries in 1902 and the couple settled into a comfortable little home. It must have appeared that he was going to lead a very stable life, as they soon started a family, which included me, Marguerite, Cecil ("Cy") and Bill.

Empress of Ireland

WE COME TO CANADA

Upon his return to England, the Colonel spent many evenings telling my father of the wonderful land he had discovered on the far side of the North American continent. He described the mighty Fraser River and how it flowed out of a narrow canyon into a broad fertile valley. I'm sure he painted quite a vivid picture of the river running between snow-capped mountain peaks to the North and through the flat valley to the South, covered with cedar, cottonwoods and of course, towering fir trees. He told father about the beautiful farm he had bought in the Fraser Valley in British Columbia, describing the farm as being "like a nest surrounded by mountains and trees". His portrayal of this new land was so intriguing that my parents decided to leave what had promised to be a comfortable life, to carve out a new life in Canada.

After selling all their furnishings and the items that could not be easily transported, they booked transatlantic passage on the lower decks of a steam ship.

In December 1908, when my brother Bill was about a month old, we sailed from Liverpool aboard the *Empress of Ireland* bound for Halifax.

Following two days at sea, we had a terrible storm. Mother became very ill and spent most of the time lying in her bunk. At first, we children were not much better off and spent more time on our backs than exploring the huge ship, but towards the end of the second day of the storm, I was beginning to feel a little better. Dad took me up for dinner.

When we entered the dining room, dishes were falling to the deck and serving trays were spilling over. We were seated, and I was served a thick soup. To keep the strange shaped bowl, which had a wide flange, from sliding off the table, the waiter put a little wooden fence around it. I must have been getting my sea legs, because I do not remember being seasick after that meal.

Once the storm blew itself out and the weather improved, I began to wander around the ship to explore. Eventually I strayed too far by going up some stairs. A lady asked me where I was from and hastily brought me back to Mom and Dad. I chuckle to think of a little ragamuffin mixing with all those high-class imperious lah-de-dahs. After two weeks at sea, we docked in Halifax where we were processed before finally boarding a train for the West.

May 1914, in thick fog, The Empress of Ireland collided with a Norwegian coal freighter within sight of the Pointe-au-Pere lighthouse in the Saint Laurence River. Some 1,012 passengers and crew perished in the disaster. This number was more than the number who went down with the Titanic in April two years earlier.

The journey from Halifax to Chilliwack, British Columbia, took about five days. Our passenger cars were equipped with hard wooden seats and the lack of comfort must have made it even more difficult for our parents on such a long journey. As we rattled through the forests of northern Ontario to the muskegs of Manitoba and across the prairies, people spread out on seats and even in the aisles for snatches of sleep.

I heard curses in many languages as short-tempered people were accidentally stepped on by passing passengers and running children. We were surrounded by fellow immigrants speaking many different languages.

I vaguely remember a small pot-bellied coal-burning stove at one end of the rail car. Some people heated food in pots and made tea in tin cans on the stove while they huddled around trying to keep warm. I also remember a man in very colourful shirt and trousers playing a violin while several men and women sang sad songs in a language I couldn't understand.

I knew the songs were sad because they had tears in their voices and some women wept into their aprons.

Smoke from the locomotive blew soot through the cars any time someone opened a door to move from coach to coach. Other smells were of pipe tobacco and so many unwashed bodies. The hopper toilets smelled whenever someone opened the door despite the fact everything fell directly to the tracks while the train was in motion. I do not remember if the railway supplied toilet paper or not. I do remember finding none and Father supplying a page of newspaper. I'm sure wealthier passengers must have travelled in more pleasant surroundings.

HARRISON

The day after Christmas, 1908, we arrived at Harrison Mills, which was just a platform by the edge of the rail-line. As the train pulled away heading for Vancouver, we were left standing alone in the wilderness. The whistle blew and I can remember a sensation like just having lost a close friend.

My father and I picked up the two suitcases while Mother carried my baby brother, Bill. Then Father led us down a long pathway to the edge of the Harrison River where a small boat waited by a floating dock. It was a sternwheeler, the "Minto", piloted by Captain Henley. After the freight and mail were loaded, we shoved off. The Harrison, a river of crystal-clear water, flowed gently on its way to join the mighty Fraser. At the mouth of the Harrison, the captain eased the bow of the sternwheeler into the muddy Fraser and turned upstream. We passed through a small channel between two gravel bars, to finally dock at Minto Landing. The journey had taken us past tall mountains that came right down to the water's edge. When we landed, I was impressed by a long set of stairs which led up the River bank to the road which I believe was the very end of Young Road North which ran straight south to Five-Corners, then on towards Sardis.

During the trip on the Minto, Captain Henley described what had been happening on the River. He explained that Jack Harrison owned two stern-wheelers, having lost a third in an unfortunate accident.

The one we were on was called *The Minto*, which basically serviced the rail station near Harrison Mills to Minto Landing. The other one operated from New Westminster to Minto Landing but no further. Other boats called *The Beaver* and *The Skeeena* operated from New Westminster up as far as Yale. Some time previously, there had also been one or two American sternwheelers that came to work on the river, because there was so much business that it could not be handled by just *The Beaver*, *The Skeeena* and a sternwheeler that Jack Harrison also operated from New Westminster to Yale. All the boats were in the habit of racing one another up the river. The fastest boat would naturally get the most passengers.

In an effort to be first, the captain of Mr. Harrison's vessel convinced the engineer to tighten down the relief-valve on the boiler, thereby increasing steam-pressure. This did give him more speed but only until the boiler could take it no longer and, somewhere around Hope, the boiler blew. According to Captain Henley, the Captain was last seen flying from the pilothouse into the water. His body was never recovered.

Another story Captain Henley told us was about a similar rivalry between Captain Johnson of the Hudson Bay's *Mount Royal*, and Captain Bonser of the *Hazelton*. Their competition on the Hazelton River grew so intense that, when the *Hazelton* rammed the *Mount Royal* during a race up river, Captain Johnson fired his rifle over the bow of the offending vessel, causing great delight to the passengers of both vessels. The Hudson's Bay offered Robert Cunningham $2500 a year for three years to remove his vessel from the Skeena run. They would even haul his freight for free in the bargain, with an option to purchase the *Hazelton*.

Three years later, in 1907, the *Mount Royal* would sink in Kitselas Canyon, drowning six crewmen and the Hudson's Bay Company would exercise their option to purchase the *Hazelton* while a replacement vessel, the *Port Simpson*, was being built. Such was life and transport on the fast-flowing rivers of British Columbia.

We got off the ferry at Minto Landing and climbed a set of stairs to where a team of horses stood hooked to a Democrat. This was a wagon with a cover on top and small curtains all around the edge.

On the way to Chilliwack, we passed many tall black stumps of trees. Later I was to learn that the "fallers" had to climb part way up some of the trees and insert springboards, because their saws were not long enough to cut through the flared portion of the trunks. Also, the wood in the lower portion of the trunk was not considered very valuable because the grain was not absolutely straight like that of the rest of the tree. For this reason, the stumps were quite tall.

We arrived at a rather desperate time for the community. Since the Harrison River Mills Timber and Trading Company had burned down in 1903, the lumber business had slowed, putting many people out of work. Now everyone was looking forward to a new mill to be opened within another year.

The Rat Portage Lumber Company opened one of B.C.'s biggest lumber mills in 1909.

The Harrison House

Mother noticed that, even though it was now winter and we had seen much snow and ice while travelling across Canada, there were still apples on some of the trees. No matter how hard our life might become, this was indeed a wonderful country and a beautiful valley. Father however, was not so impressed. From the time we had arrived in Chilliwack it had been raining and the streets and boardwalks were a sea of mud. No matter, we spent several days at *The Harrison House* where Mrs. Harrison did a wonderful job of making us feel at home.

Following our stay in Mrs. Harrison's boarding house, we moved to a small cabin on Menzies Street. The cabin was really a shack with exposed 2"x4" studding, supporting 1"x12" rough boards and no siding over the rough boards.

That winter was one of the coldest I'd ever spent in my life thus far. Our only source of heat was the cook-stove, which we kept going all the time. When the temperature outside dropped to well below zero, and the cook-stove was being fed continuously, the boards on the side of the cabin started to dry out and shrink. The cabin was soon so drafty that it became increasingly difficult to keep warm. I can remember Mother taking old rags and paper to stuff the cracks; a never-ending job all through that first winter.

Colonel Coote, who had bought his farm not far away from where we were, helped Father get a job as night-policeman in Chilliwack. In those days there was a curfew in town; children under a certain age were not allowed to be out on the streets alone after 9 p.m. My father carried a shillelagh with him on his rounds and if he caught any young person vandalizing or causing mischief, justice was swiftly administered. The young offenders would then be taken home to their parents, where further discipline usually awaited. The curfew and the acceptance of immediate corporal punishment kept vandalism to a minimum.

The shillelagh was a stout knotty walking stick with a large knob at the top.

Father was to keep that position for several years or at least until he was able to switch to the day shift.

Once Father was on the day shift, our evenings would be spent listening to the stories he had picked up about the area in which we now lived. He told us about the Scowlitz and Sts'Ailes or Chehalis people who had lived in longhouses until the missionaries separated them into smaller families. The Sts'Ailes, whose name means "beating heart" told stories of giant men called "Sasquatch" who lived in the forests around Harrison Bay. The Sasquatch is sacred and is the emblem of the Chehalis people.

Many of the tallest Douglas fir along the Chehalis River had been cut down by the Canadian Pacific Railway to build railway bridges and now the Sasquatch even came into town after dark because the white men had destroyed their homes. These stories, as we grew older, were supposed to keep us from wanting to go out after dark. Later, when the almost new Rat Portage Lumber Company sawmill at Harrison Mills was shut down in 1912, some people rumoured it was because of the Sasquatch. Some people still claim to see the Sasquatch around Harrison Mills, even to this day.

Father also told us about the Sumas who built fishing villages on reed stilts on Sumas Lake to escape the swarms of mosquitoes while fishing for sturgeon and hunting ducks and geese to feed their families through the winter months.

> *The B.C. government would drain the lake in the 1920's to control flooding. The sturgeon would die in the mud while non-Native settlers were able to buy the rich farmland for between $60 to $120 an acre.*

I loved the outdoors and did whatever I could to be helpful around the house. I remember a spring day when I decided to help my mother by splitting wood for the fire. I made my way out to the chopping block, picked up the axe and tried to split a piece of wood. Cecil, my younger brother, had followed me out. When the piece of wood toppled from the chopping block, Cecil attempted to help me by bending down to pick it up and place it back on the chopping block. I was in the process of taking another swing with the axe when his head came up. He received a small cut, which sent him screaming to mother who patched him up and put a quick end to my woodcutting. Thinking back, it must have been very stressful for a mother with young boys and so many sharp farm and logging implements around.

As winter passed, we had a few more nasty cold spells and Father decided enough was enough. We would have to have better lodging before the beginning of the next cold season. By spring, he bought two lots on Lewis Avenue and made arrangements to start building a house. Father hired a carpenter by the name of Tom

Hepburn, to help him build a two-story house with proper siding. The house would be finished with plaster walls inside. In those days, effective insulation was not available. At least the new house was not drafty as it had been in the old shack, and provided a great improvement in comfort over our first winter there.

Just behind the house, Dad built a woodshed with a covered walkway to the back door. It would keep the rain and snow off the wood. By fall, the house was completed and we moved in.

Along with the new house came a new chore for me. Mine was the daily task of filling the wood box by the kitchen stove. The covered walkway also proved to be a good place for hanging pheasants, ducks, geese, and grouse that Dad would shoot. Whenever we had three or four birds hanging there, Mother would get me and my sister Marguerite to help pluck the birds.

She would cook them, remove all the meat and put the bones in a large pot to make soup. Then she would can the meat in jars. This meat was to make lunches for us when we went to school. Dad was a good hunter and always had lots of wild game hanging by the shed. Along with our vegetable garden, we sustained ourselves very nicely.

In 1910, both grandparents decided to join my parents and the grandchildren in Canada. Within a few years, the entire Carey clan had migrated to the Fraser Valley. We were all living in the Chilliwack area.

Chilliwhyeuk in the language of the Halq'eméylem language means "as far upriver as you can go before having to switch to a pole".

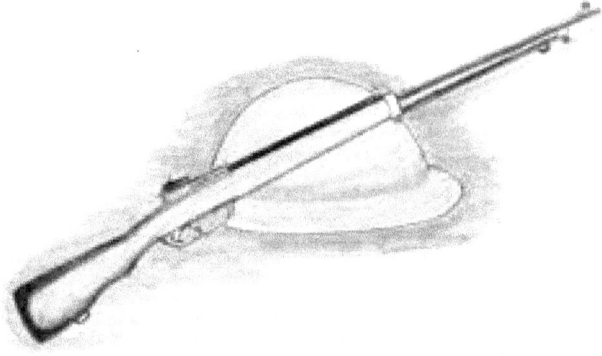

THE GREAT WAR

Father remained with the police force until about 1913 when he decided to try some other jobs, however, I don't think they turned out very well. Father was still following his military career as a reservist. He was in the 104th Regiment, so when the war broke out in 1914, he joined the 47th Battalion in New Westminster.

The 47th Battalion of the Canadian Expeditionary Forces took part in many major battles including Amiens, Ypres, Vimy, Hill 60, Valenciennes, Canal du Nord and Passchendaele.

After settling things with Mother, Father was sent overseas. This left Mother with three boys and a girl to look after on her own. It took about six months before Dad's paycheques began arriving from the government. Until that time, in order to keep up the payments on the house and the lot, Mother had to work in the fire hall as a cook. This she did for several months.

Since, among other things, we learned gardening in the school gardens, we children took on the family vegetable garden, growing cabbages, potatoes, carrots, onions and many of the staples that kept us going when other foods began to run out. Our parents were told the school gardens were intended to teach us observation for drawing and other school subjects. Certainly, I enjoyed digging and planting, even weeding with a hoe, much more than drawing, history or spelling. On the other hand, I did well at arithmetic and geography. Those subjects would serve me well in later years.

Just before going overseas, Father had made application for a homestead of 147 acres on an island in the Fraser River. Like many other servicemen, he had received verbal assurance from the department in charge of homesteads that his time overseas would count towards the time required to develop the property and that this would most likely qualify him, upon his return, for the title or deed.

Of course, with Father gone, there was no more wild game hanging in the passageway to the woodshed. My brother Cy managed to work part-time for *Jub and Stallard*, who had a butcher shop and an abattoir in town. Sometimes they would give him a beef-head to bring home. Then it would be my job to skin the head, remove the tongue, take the eyes out, and split the head open. Mother would clean this all up, put the head in a pot and boil it to remove the meat. The rest, she would use to make very tasty headcheese.

In time, Mother also bought a couple of cows to supply us with milk. She would put some of the milk in a cool place in order to let the cream rise to the top. Then she would separate the cream and churn it to make butter. Since she did not have a butter churn, Mother improvised by putting the cream in a one or two-quart sealer along with a coin about the size of a fifty cent piece, and securing the lid, she would hold the top of the jar with one hand and the bottom with the other and bounce the jar from knee to knee, to move the coin up and down through the cream. This method was very effective for making butter. We children always got to drink the delicious buttermilk when she was finished.

Father was wounded, and finally returned home in 1918. He took a job as a Forest Ranger around Chilliwack Lake. Because we now had six cows, Father decided we would be far better off on a farm. He went to the land office to claim his homestead, but, despite his war service, the verbal assurance that he had been given no longer stood.

He was still required to have a building on the property and at least four acres fully cleared plus four acres roughly cleared. Since this part had not been accomplished, his application for the piece of land was denied. However, through the Soldier Settlement Act of 1919, Dad was able to get a loan to buy 94 acres at the end of Jefferson Road on Rose Island. The lower part had a section-house on it, with an apple orchard and about four acres of cleared land.

A section house was a small two-room structure built to house railroad workers who looked after sections of railway line. The house upriver had only about half an acre cleared around it.

CLEARING THE LAND

Father sold the house on Lewis Avenue and began making payments on the new farm. Mother, Dad and now two girls, stayed in one cabin and we boys lived in the other. That spring, Father went to his new job as a fire ranger up around the Chilliwack Lake District, and left us boys to clear the land for planting and to develop pasture for the cows. We got to work and were soon able to put in a garden. We were hardy in those days. Cy was eleven, I was ten, Bill was five.

While clearing some maple stumps, we came across a huge black-hornets' nest. We decided to knock it down and burn it that night, when all the hornets would be inside. Cy's Cocker Spaniel had been taught to retrieve. Without thinking, we proceeded to throw sticks at the nest to knock it down. The Cocker Spaniel ran in after one of the sticks and came yelping back followed by a storm of hornets. The dog ran straight for Cy and the hornets followed. We took off for the house as fast as we could. We were not as fast as the Cocker Spaniel, nor the hornets that pursued. Cy got stung several times. That night we carefully crept up to the nest and poured coal oil around and over it, and set it on fire.

Cy got a job for a few days on a neighboring farm and used the money to buy stumping-powder, caps and fuse-line. We bought an auger for drilling into the stumps and underneath them. After the stumps were blown to bits, we used a team of horses to pull what remained off to one side. When Father came back in the Fall, he was surprised that we had been able to clean up so much land and get the stumps out.

We didn't have much money back then, but once in a while, Charlie Seymour, one of the local Natives, would bring us a salmon in trade for vegetables. We were quite happy with our lot. In the late fall, Father would take one of us boys up the mountain to hunt for deer.

In that way, we had meat with our vegetables. Whoever got to go hunting with Dad, was given the opportunity to grow even closer to the man who helped bring so much love into our lives and who had so much living experience to share with each of us. Although he never said much about his experiences in Europe, he loved to tell stories about his days in China and India. The Great War was too painful to share and remained bottled up inside my father for the remainder of his life.

Mother used to cut the deer meat into pieces and can it so that we had meat throughout the winter.

Sometimes, however, we would still run out of food and had to live on rolled oats until a milk cheque came in. No matter how difficult times could be, mother always remained cheerful and reminded us to be thankful for what we had.

That first fall on the farm, we also began cutting-up maple logs and hauling the cordwood six miles into town where we would sell our logs for four dollars a cord. We would then bring back hay and oats for the horses so we could haul in more cords of wood. All winter we sold cordwood and cleared the land. Much of our spare time was spent pulling stumps and hauling them off to the side. Sometimes we would get work on one of the neighboring farms, putting corn into the silos. This would give us extra money to help us through the winter months. At other times, we made money by cutting wood on other people's properties. We sure kept ourselves busy.

One weekend the following spring, Dad was taking Bill upriver to hunt for deer. On the way, they passed a logjam. There, in the middle of the logjam was a length of brand new 12" x 12" beam. This was exactly what we needed to build a new hay barn and a new cow barn. The next morning, the three of us headed up river and pulled that timber out and towed it back to where we planned to build the barn.

At about this time, my brothers and I decided to pool our savings to buy an Indian dugout canoe. We would put this to good use searching the riverbanks and logjams for more timbers. It was surprising how much building material could be obtained from the river.

Father went out with the canoe one morning to a logjam not very far up river from the property. He found another brand new 12" x 12" about twenty-four feet long and came back for the three of us. Soon we were wrestling that timber out of the jam.

We had just gotten the piece free, when the whole pile of logs began to break-up and there were logs floating down river all around us. We managed to get back to the canoe with our tools but had to let that timber go down river with the rest of the trees, logs and debris. After that, we went up to some of the islands to get cedar poles for the uprights. We squared off the corner-poles and notched them to put the vertical boards up. Then we used 1x12 lumber for the siding. From the river we obtained enough good cedar, from which we split shakes for the roof. Once we got the hay-barn finished, Father bought a rig for lifting hay off the hay-wagon and into the barn. Our next project was to build the cow barn.

LOGGING COTTONWOOD

We heard we could sell cottonwood bolts in Washington State. *Bolts are the straight timbers from cottonwood trees, usually 15 to 18 inches in diameter.* We started logging the cottonwood, using one of those old two-man crosscut saws; however, we soon discovered one of us would have to learn how to sharpen the saws for falling and bucking logs. I knew an elderly man who had been filing saws in a logging camp, so I went to see him and got him to teach me how to set a saw up to sharpen it, how to joint it, how to set the teeth, and how to set the rakers. He showed me the different tools I would need. I then went to town and bought a swedging-hammer – a hammer with a half-pound head.

I also bought a swedging-block, a raker-gauge, and a spider. Then I returned home and started sharpening saws.

> *A raker is a tooth set that has a uniform set angle and a three tooth set sequence of left, right, and straight. A spider is a gauge used to determine when the set is correct. (Crosscut Saw manual).*

One had to be very careful not to file too much because all the teeth had to be the same length and the rakers had to be just down a fraction from the point of the cutting teeth. I picked up the skill fairly quickly. We were then able to fall the trees and cut the cottonwood into lengths, without constantly having to take the saw in to a saw filer. This saved both the expense of the service plus the time that would have been wasted in constantly taking the saw into town.

When we had shipped a couple of loads of cottonwood to Everett on the railcars, Dad bought a McGregor Drag-Saw. This saw was no good for falling a tree, but quite useful in cutting the tree trunk to whatever lengths we desired. It was the type of saw that preceded the chainsaw. Basically it included a gasoline engine, which drove a crank arm. The crank arm was attached to something very similar to a one-man crosscut saw blade. The whole contraption was mounted on a rather cumbersome frame. When the motor was running, the crank arm would push the saw blade back and forth to cut its way through the tree trunk. Because of its bulk and weight, it usually took the two of us to move it around and place it for each new cut. The effort was worthwhile because, once it was operating, it did save us a lot of backbreaking work that we'd otherwise have to do with the old two-man crosscut saw.

We would cut the cottonwood into four-foot-six lengths, split it into bolts, remove any bark that remained, and let the logs dry for a while. Wood was sold by the cord, which was the measure of a volume of wood being a stack four feet high, four feet wide and eight feet long. By having us cut the wood in four foot six inches lengths, the buyer got a bit more than a cord of wood for his money.

When we had about twenty cords, I would haul it all out to the railway siding using a wagon and team of horses. Each boxcar would take seventeen, eighteen, maybe twenty cords of wood. It would usually take two or three of us all day, from early morning, to load that boxcar. At the most we would only have a couple of days to load our wood, because those cars had to be out of the siding within two days. If the boxcars were tied up for longer than forty-eight hours, we would have to pay a demurrage fee. We only had to pay once.

Everett was not the only customer we had. We also shipped a lot of cottonwood in bolt form to a company by the name of *Restmore* in Vancouver.

I believe most of the wood was turned into excelsior, a wood straw used for packaging fragile items and for stuffing mattresses.

By logging the cottonwood, we were killing two birds with one stone. The sale of the wood brought in much-needed cash to help pay off the V.L.A. loan, and more of the farm was cleared. Of course the stumps still remained to be removed using stumping powder and good old-fashioned muscle-power. They then could be dragged off to the side to be burnt at our leisure. The odd time, enough powder would be used to "over loosen" the stump and although it was gratifying to see the stump flying through the air, it was a waste of expensive stumping powder!

BEES AND HONEY

Most of the cottonwood trees we felled were about four feet in diameter. Sometimes they would be five feet. We hit one that measured six feet. Since we had an eight-foot crosscut saw, so it took us quite a while to bring that tree down.

We cleared an area where we wanted the tree to fall, but we didn't clear far enough. Part of the tree fell into the bush. When that tree came down, we heard a buzzing sound near the top of the tree. We went to investigate, but had to leave in a hurry because some honeybees had established themselves in a hollow in the top of the tree.

The next day the bees took off to look for another hollow tree. They hovered above the stump for a while then disappeared. When we cut open the top part of that tree, we found quite a large quantity of honeycomb with honey in it. It was fresh golden in colour and some of it was very old, indicating that the bees had been in that tree for quite some time. When we finally rendered it all out, we had about fifty to sixty pounds of delicious honey. We boiled the honey to separate the wax. The honey was put in jars and we had sweetener for our porridge in the mornings. We also had wax for mother to make candles.

Later that summer, a swarm of bees came along and settled in a maple tree, on a branch about twelve feet off the ground. Cy wanted to get those bees into a box. We'd seen hives before but we really didn't know anything about them. Cy built a box with a movable lid and cut a hole in front, for the bees to go in and out. Then he climbed up and sat on the limb, and started cutting that limb with a handsaw. Finally, the limb broke, but it didn't fall all the way to the ground. It just swung beneath him, with bees swarming all around. Cy had to sit very quietly for a long while, until those bees settled down. Then he tried sawing some more.

Later, we took a rope and tied it around the branch. Finally, we were able to lower the branch and bees gently to the ground. We put some paper in front of the box to attract the bees and those bees walked quietly into the hive, just like an army on the march. That evening we closed the entrance to the box and carried the hive close to the house.

We got one harvest of honey out of that box, before the colony died the following winter.

CHARLIE SEYMOUR

Charlie Seymour was a Native from the Chehailus River Reserve. Sometimes he would come by and set up his camp just a little way down the river from us. In the evening we would go over to visit, and he would tell us stories about the old days.

Charlie showed us a spear he used for catching salmon. He showed us how it worked. It had a central spear with two large-size barbs on the outside sections. It also had a thong that he could pull up once he had hooked a fish. When he speared a salmon, the two outside parts would hook right in and hold the fish tight. For night fishing, Charlie taught us how to build a container for fire, to be held in place over the side of the canoe with a metal plate and some sticks.

We paddled up to the head of the rapids, lit our fire, which Charlie had helped us build, and allowed the canoe to drift. My brother Bill knelt ready with his spear. A salmon came up and Bill jabbed at it but missed. Then another came up and he missed that one too. Finally, he jabbed at another fish and caught it. Well, it must have been a sturgeon, because it made such a splash that next thing we knew we were all in the water. We held on to the canoe and drifted down to the bottom of the rapids, where we could get the canoe ashore. Bill had to swim out and retrieve his paddle.

When we got ashore, there were some other Native people there and, when they found out what had happened, they all began to laugh and talk in their own language. We took off our wet clothes and wrung them out to dry as well as we could, and got the canoe back in order.

We knew there wouldn't be much use trying to go back to fishing. Anyway, Charley gave us a couple of salmon to take home with us.

We got into our canoe and began paddling, arriving home at about 2.30 in the morning. We put the two salmon in the outside cooler before going to our bunks. Next morning, we were up and busy with our chores. When we got in for breakfast, we told Mother what had happened, but she didn't seem to be too worried. She knew by then we were capable of looking after ourselves. Mother never had to worry that we'd be up to mischief or running around in town. We had too many responsibilities to even think of wasting our time. Besides, we had much more fun being in the fresh air and making new discoveries.

CANOE SAILING

Some Natives had come down from up near Hope, to spear salmon at Chehailus Rapids. We noticed they had put sails on their canoes and were whipping along in the wind, making really good time. Bill and I thought this was a great idea and decided to make a sail for our canoe. However, we thought we'd make one bigger so we'd go faster. That was a bad mistake.

Our mast was about five times too big and the sail was twice the size that it should have been for the canoe. This we found out very quickly, when the wind grew stronger and we decided to try our sail out.

We were in a back-eddy, and when the wind caught that sail, it just made our canoe leap out into the fast water. The nose swung around and the wind caught the sail. Next thing we knew, we were in the water. After that, we decided we would make a sail the same size as the ones the Natives were using, and not any bigger. We made a small mast and used a bed-sheet for a sail. We practiced sailing until we were doing as well as anyone else on the river.

Early one morning, Mother came to me and said: "We're out of flour and I need some soda and baking-powder and cream of tartar." Since we had no wood ready to haul, I didn't see a need to hitch up the horses, so I decided I'd just take the canoe and go down the Fraser to Minto Landing and walk into town from there.

I'd bring a pack with me and bring back what Mother needed. Well, that sack of flour was so heavy on that long walk, I had to stop and rest three times, before I got back to the canoe. Once in the canoe, there was a good breeze and I covered the flour up with my jacket so it wouldn't get wet. Before too long I was back home. That sail worked pretty well.

In the fall, Cecil, Bill and I used to go to work for the local farmers. I saved my money and finally had enough to buy a motorboat. I bought one that was all closed in with a ten horsepower one-cylinder motor. It wasn't a very fast boat, but we enjoyed doing work with it and getting up and down the river whenever we had the chance.

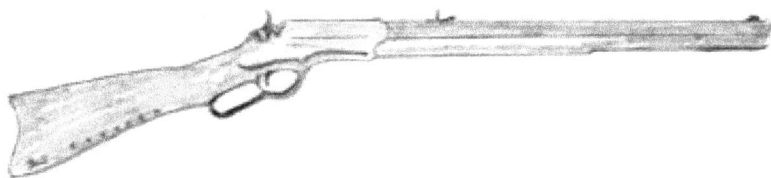

DEER HUNTING

I was digging stumps again and Johnny Jess, a neighbour who lived about a mile from us, came up to me and said: "I hear there's a lot of deer up on Long Island. Why don't we go up and get us a few?" Well, I thought that was a good idea. So Johnny and a fellow by the name of Mr. Brown brought along their sleeping gear and a few items of food. I got the gas and filled up the tank in the boat, and away we went.

We travelled down the Fraser, to the Harrison River. We had quite a time getting up the Chehailus Rapids, because they run so fast, however, we finally made it into the lake. Then we followed the west side of the lake until we came to Long Island. There, we found a nice cove with an entrance that was protected from the North and from just about any direction the wind would want to blow. Johnny told us he knew of a cabin close by that a friend had told him about. Sure enough, we found the cabin. The door had been left open, but nothing was damaged. We had to cut some firewood, and made sure to have enough to leave some for the next people who might want to stay over. We cut cedar and fir boughs to make mattresses for the three bunks that were in the cabin, and got settled-in for the night.

The next morning we rose early to find that it had snowed about four inches during the night. I was

35

wearing soft shoes so as to be quieter in the woods than I would have been with boots on. However, I went along. We saw a couple of doe, but we didn't want to shoot those. We were only going to shoot bucks.

This way, there would always be more deer in the future. We knew quite a bit about conservation back then. I finally went back to the cabin. My feet were so cold, I could hardly walk. Before long the other two boys came back with a deer each.

Another morning and we were set to return home but the wind was so strong we couldn't get out of there. If the motor on the boat were to stop, we would end up on the rocks in no time. Later the next day the wind had calmed down enough that we thought we had better try heading home. The going was quite rough, and by the time we reached where the lake met the river, we thought we had better stop for the night. We slept on the rocks, getting on our way as soon as there was sufficient light.

When we got home, we skinned the two deer. Then we cut the meat into quarters. Mother separated the meat from the bones and we cut it into smaller pieces for canning. Canning required boiling the meat for four hours in the jars in a big boiler. This job took another two days, but the meat would last all winter.

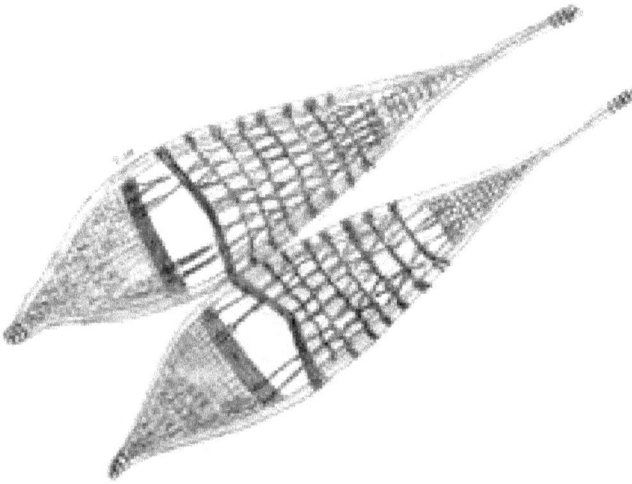

SNOWSHOES

One winter we had quite a lot of snow. Our friend Charlie Seymour showed us how to make snowshoes. We cut Maple strips about as long as we were tall, using only the sapwood or outer rings of the limbs and making sure the grain was exceptionally straight throughout each strip. Once we cut the pieces to shape, we steamed them over a hot fire until the pieces became quite pliable.

Then we joined each rounded strip at the bottom with black bear-hide, which had the fur removed and secured two cross pieces in each to hold the centers apart. Once the wood cooled, the rims kept their shape ready to be woven with strips of bear hide. The hard part was drilling holes all around through which we could lace and tie the long bear-hide strips. When we were finished, Charlie gave us some sticky tree sap to bond everything together. Our three pairs of snowshoes lasted us through three winters before some of the bear-hide strips had to be replaced.

THE SPEEDBOAT

An unemployed gentleman used to drop by and talk with us once in a while. Sometimes, he'd help us getting a stump out. Sometimes, he liked to just sit and chat. One sunny afternoon, he told me he wanted to buy my boat. I hadn't thought of selling. He wanted to sail up the Harrison to see if he could find work in one of the logging camps. The fellow had been unemployed for more than two years and had earned his way doing odd jobs. I agreed that if he would give me what I had paid for it, I would sell him the boat. He paid me my hundred dollars and equipped the boat with a Coleman stove, a small bunk, all his provisions and gas for the motor, and off he went.

Late the following spring, he came back to see us. He told us that at one logging camp there wouldn't be a job for him for three months. After circling the lake and failing to find work at any of the other camps, he decided to go down the Fraser to the ocean and see if he could get a better job in one of the logging camps up the Coast. After his visit, he took off and that was the last we ever saw or heard of him.

In the meantime, I found another boat for sale. This one was a speedboat, about twenty-four feet long. This was a bigger boat than the last one, and I got it for about the same price I had received for my first boat. I thought I had done quite well for myself, until I discovered the motor was just about worn out. Fortunately for me, someone had driven a large six-cylinder Juett motorcar over the bank on Bear Mountain Road. When I found out about it, I went to the insurance company and bought salvaging rights for twenty-five dollars. Billy Farr had a truck, so he made a deal with me that he would go and bring me back the engine, if he could take all the rest of the parts of the car that he needed, such as the wheels, the rear end, the front axles and the radiator. Naturally, I agreed. I overhauled the motor and installed it in the boat.

THE HOMESTEAD

As mentioned earlier, shortly before going overseas to fight in the Great War, Dad had obtained the rights to "homestead" one hundred and forty acres on an island about a mile-and-a-half further up river.

When Dad had failed to satisfy the requirements of the Homesteading Act, the right to apply for the piece of land had passed to another man who had not signed up to fight for his country. Of course, in our travels up and down the river, we would pass by the island now and then. At no time did we ever notice any activity. It was becoming apparent that the new applicant would likewise fail to satisfy the requirements of the Act. I discussed this with Dad and indicated that I would like to see if anything at the site had been done or not.

The following Sunday I discovered, to my delight, nothing had been done. Dad had lost interest in the property and told me he did not intend to reapply. I asked him if it would be a good plan for me to go into New Westminster and make application on the homestead, in my name, so that we could reclaim it.

When Dad agreed, I travelled to New Westminster, and was able to make out an application, "pending inspection of the property".

After a couple of months, I received a letter from the government offices, giving me permission to move onto the property and to begin assessment work. I knew I would have to get busy very soon, in order to keep it.

The next weekend, my brother Bill and I went up there and began clearing the maples. We got quite a bit done on that first weekend. The regulation was that we had to have four acres cleared and cultivated and four acres in the rough, within a certain time limit. "In the rough" meant with stumps on and hay or something like that growing on the property. After several weekends, we had felled all the maples on the eight acres. The maples were cut into firewood and stacked to dry.

By then, the river was getting higher and I would have to use the canoe to get to the island. I went to town and bought some one-by-twelves and cut them into six-foot lengths. I took these up and built a small lean-to shelter where I could stay dry when it rained.

The following Friday night, I was sitting in my shelter with a small fire going and planning what had to be done next. Suddenly, a cougar let out a bloodcurdling scream. I sat up with every hair on my head standing straight on end and began to wonder if being in the wilds by myself was such a bright idea. It sure would have been nice to be back in my comfortable bed at home. Anyway, I threw a few more sticks on the fire and, after a while, my heart stopped pounding and I began to feel a bit better. I kept watch because I didn't know whether the cougar had made a kill and was protesting it with a bear, or whether he was voicing a challenge to my being in his territory. Finally, however, I fell asleep.

The next morning, I looked around but could find no trace of a cougar nor of a fresh kill. I got busy cutting more of those maples and pulling the cordwood lengths out to a clear space, away from the cottonwood trees, where I would be able to take them away when the river level went back down later in the year. I was able to cut, carry and stack about three-quarters of a cord of wood a day. The cottonwood were beautiful trees and I knew I would eventually be able to make up a boom for export to Japan.

A log boom is a series of long logs joined together in the water to surround and contain a collection of freshly harvested logs.

That first summer, the summer of '26, I spent every weekend cutting and clearing maple and brush

42

away from the cottonwood. By Fall I had about thirteen cord stacked up. I got hold of a one-ton Federal Truck and was able to drive it in by Gill Road, to the gravel bar.

That Fall I sold my wood in Chilliwack for four dollars a cord. Then I brought in enough lumber to build a small cabin, with just a kitchen and a bedroom. I was quite comfortable and felt much safer than I had sleeping in my open lean-to shelter. I never did see nor hear from that cougar again.

During the spring of 1927, I contacted an exporter who was sending cottonwood logs across the Pacific, and arranged for a shipment to China. I brought in boom chains and borrowed an auger to bore a four-inch hole in the end of each boom-stick. That summer I got out one good-sized boom of about fifty thousand board feet. These were all short logs of eight to sixteen feet. We couldn't go over sixteen feet for export. Also we couldn't go over twenty-four inches at the top end but could go as low as eight inches. This was good for me, so I was able to get along pretty well on my own. When I had the boom ready, I got in touch with Charlie Merchant, who ran a tugboat out of Mission. He came up and took the tow down to New Westminster for me.

The Fraser Valley has always been the home to the Bald Eagle. Sometimes I'd lie on my back and watch dozens of those majestic birds ride the thermals above the Fraser River. Then, my mind would turn to flying. I knew, however, if ever I was going to own an aircraft, I would first have to find a way to make and save money. I made up my mind to complete the requirements of the Homestead Act, in order to secure the title to the land I had already put so much labour into. Meanwhile, there was neither time nor money for anything but the property. Three years would pass, and a lot of hard work, before I would receive the title to my own farm. Just about the time I finally became a landowner, the depression struck. If it had been difficult in the past to save money for flying lessons, it was to prove almost impossible to do so for many years to come.

Still, I pressed on with dogged determination. The farm itself was not yet developed far enough to be profitable, but I was still able to cut cottonwood bolts and other varieties of wood for firewood. These I could sell for four dollars a cord.

I managed to get four or five booms assembled and towed them down to New Westminster with the speedboat that I'd fixed up. It was much more convenient, using my own boat, because I didn't have to wait for a tugboat. The expense of operating my own boat was much less than what I would otherwise have to pay.

When the weather was suitable for logging, I had to put my dreams of flying aside. I would need money for flying lessons and there was a tremendous amount of work to do on the new farm. Still, the only method of gaining extra cash was to cut hardwood for sale.

Earlier on in the winter, I had learned that the instructor at the *Cokaleetsa Indian School* in Sardis had just finished building a tug for Harold Cartnell. It was a good method of providing the young Native men with hands-on experience in the boat building trade. Although they had built one boat, they were hoping to build one more to give a few more students some trade experience. I went out and talked to the instructor. Basically all they wanted me to do was supply the necessary materials and they would build a boat, which would be mine once it was completed. There would be no extra charge for labour because they were happy to have materials supplied free of charge on which to practice boat building.

Harold had given his boat the name Cokaleetsa No.1. Mine was launched later in the spring with the name Cokaleetsa No.2. I picked up a second-hand Marine motor from Charlie Gardiner, which I rebuilt and fitted into the boat. Now I had a vessel capable of earning its keep and possibly making me some real money.

That summer, I got out one or two booms and started towing on the river for other loggers. I made several trips up river to a place just below Yale. The loggers were bringing wood out from the Kohakella River.

Other people who towed booms from this area would bring the booms through the Pertain Rapids just below Hope. This was an area of fast water where the Fraser River crossed the valley up to a mountainside, suddenly turning 90 degrees and causing treacherous currents and whirlpools.

Most of the towboats would release their booms at the beginning of the rapids and pick them up down river, if the booms got through in one piece. Sometimes the booms would break up so badly there would not be much to hook onto. I thought that if a few booms could make it through intact, it might be possible to actually tow the booms through and hopefully direct them away from the steep mountain cliff where the river turned.

I told my deckhand what I had in mind and instructed him to stand by the tow-bit with an axe. If it looked as though we were going to get into serious trouble, I was going to have him cut the towrope.

We started down the rapids and passed by one whirlpool on the left hand side. We had gone a little too close to the whirlpool, because part of the boom became caught and a couple of logs were pulled down. They popped back to the surface at least 20 feet away from the boom. Despite that, we had made it through, and the rest of the trip to New Westminster was quite tame in comparison.

Since I had taken the boom to New Westminster successfully, it was easier to get more customers for my towing services from that area. I made several trips that summer for different loggers in the area.

In January 1938 I began to cut and drag cottonwood from the farm until I had five booms ready. Then I towed those booms down to New Westminster. The wood was intended to be exported to Japan, but nobody had told me the Japanese boats that had been hauling cottonwood were now busy hauling scrap-iron. The market for cottonwood had dried up and I could not find another buyer for the wood.

Cottonwood doesn't float for very long before it becomes waterlogged and sinks. I lost my five booms with all the boom chains and *swifters*, and was left with huge bills for fuel, food and wages. I managed to pay off the men, but I still had to make up the rest of the money.

I found work for my tugboat at Port Mellon with a Mr. Haskell, who was running a sawmill and shipping lumber. I used my boat to tow small booms from a holding-pen to where we would break them up and send the logs into the mill. I worked at Port Mellon all summer until Mr. Haskell closed down. During all that time, I had been flying whenever possible but still didn't have enough money to pay for an instructor's licence. In the summer of 1938, I decided to take a big leap. I sold the homestead on the island and paid off most of the outstanding bills.

When the Port Mellon sawmill closed down, I went to work at Rainy River on the booming ground. The pay was better than I'd earned anywhere else. After a couple of months, I had not only paid of the balance I owed, I even had enough cash saved up to go back to Vancouver and get my certificate. The day I informed the supervisor of the booming ground I was leaving to pursue a new career, he laughed and told me he figured I would be no different from the rest of the men who worked the camps along the B.C. Coast. He was sure I would spend my bankroll in one or two weeks, having a grand time in Vancouver. He was so confident he was right he said I could have my job back when I returned.

BOOMING GROUND PROBLEMS

I'll jump ahead in time to tell you about the next time I returned to log booming. It was during a brief break between aviation jobs sometime in 1943.

Of course I loved flying by that time but sometimes it was necessary to find jobs that paid better than flying during those war years.

Bert Tremblay was a forestry engineer working for Columbia Cellulose near Terrace, B.C. He was surveying timber logs going to the mill and having trouble with his boom-men. They weren't getting their work done.

The company was going to dump the logs into the Skeena River at high water. They had to have the booming-ground ready, or the logs would go on down past Telegraph Point to the ocean.

Telegraph Point, at that time, was used as a communications point for navigation, although it is no longer known as such.

Bert asked me if I had ever boomed in fast water. He made me such a good offer I agreed to work for him. We were using dolphins. A dolphin consists of one centre-pile driven into the riverbed, with several other piles driven around it, and the whole thing lashed together with a cable. We had to put in between half to three quarters of a mile of sheer boom. The men he had working for him were only completing about three sticks a day. No way would that boom be ready on time. When he finally fired the other workers,

I told the boss my brother was a good boom-man and I also knew of an elderly French-Canadian by the name of Colby who would be a good worker.

It is interesting to note that quite a few French-speaking Canadians have English or Irish names. Many had been adopted as orphans by Quebec families after coming to Canada from Ireland during the potato famine and following the death of so many of the immigrants from typhoid during that tragic year of 1847.

A great number of those people, many of whom were Irish, lie buried on the quarantine island of Grosse Isle, upstream from Quebec City. Following its recognition as a national historic site in 1974, a commemorative plaque was laid in 1980, paying tribute to the role of Grosse Isle as a quarantine station, especially during the cholera and typhus epidemics which marked the first half of the 19th century.

We had to bore holes into each end of the boom-sticks and pull the chains through the holes before attaching a link like a shackle. We heated the end of the link and riveted it so that it wouldn't come undone. The three of us were turning out twenty to thirty boom-sticks a day.

Pretty soon I was ready and the company sent a towboat in to tie them to the dolphins. This had to be done at high-water slack. "High-water-slack" occurs at the lower end of the river when the tide starts to recede and the river returns to its normal flow. When everything was ready we had a safety-wire we put around to make sure nothing would come undone.

This took about two-and-a-half weeks, and we had everything ready. Next, we had the booming ground to set up. Columbia Cellulose sent a boat in with the boom-sticks and we had to lace the area for the tide coming in and for the tide going out.

We got a few booms out that summer, then the river began to freeze up and I had to radio to report one of the booms was frozen in the ice. The company sent a tug up that day and we took some caps and powder and broke up the ice to get the boom out. Then the ice got worse and we had to wait for a while. Finally the ice got so bad that the company came and took us out.

I had been studying heavy-duty diesel engineering for over a year-and-a-half. I was thinking about going to school in Edmonton to take my practical course and my exams and then I'd have my engineering ticket. However, that winter the ice took all the dolphins out so the following spring the company sent up a pile driver and we put all the dolphins back in. We located all the boom-sticks that had been torn out by the ice, and repaired what damage had been done. Then we set everything back in place and started work.

I told Mr. Tremblay I wanted to put the boom-sticks on the upper side of the dolphins because otherwise big logs would come down and push smaller logs under the boom-sticks, and we were losing quite a few logs that way. However, Mr. Tremblay didn't agree. We worked all that summer and into the late fall. That winter, the ice took the dolphins out for a second time.

50

Columbia Cellulose thought they were losing too much money for what they were getting, so they closed the camp down. Soon after that, I went back to what I loved best, flying.

PART TWO

FLYING WITH EAGLES

FLYING WITH THE FLEDGLINGS

In the spring of 1910, when I was seven years old, I listened to Colonel Coote talking with my dad about Charles Hamilton and his flying machine travelling through the air like a bird from Lulu Island, (Richmond) to New Westminster and back, a distance of 20 miles in only 30 minutes. The colonel was interested because he told my dad he considered flying machines would be very useful if ever there was another war. That same year, 1910, William Gibson of Victoria began experimenting with his own flying machine but people were laughing at him and saying he'd never get anywhere although he actually flew several times the following year.

Then some fellows in Vancouver built their own flying machine with an engine from the United States. They lost their machine in a fire. In 1911, Billy Stark, a Vancouver auto racer, went to California to learn about flying from Glenn Curtiss, who built *airoplanes* and was giving flying lessons. Billy returned to British Columbia with a pilot's licence. In April, 1912, the *Daily Province* printed a story about flying with Billy Stark in his Curtiss "Flyer." Father expressed some interest until

Stark was injured late in 1912. At about that time, I sprained my ankle jumping from the hay barn into a pile of hay. I wanted to see what it would be like to fly through the air like Billy Stark.

Father told us boys, flying was far more dangerous than jumping from barns and we should stay away. Still, I knew the day would come when I too would fly, maybe even in my own flying machine.

By 1919, William E Boeing and Eddie Hubbard were carrying international airmail between Vancouver and Seattle using a Boeing-built C2 seaplane while Captain Ernest Hoy, a former RAF pilot had flown from Vancouver to Calgary that August. Ten years later, with the start of the Depression, many pilots who had flown with the Royal Air Force during the war were now flying around the province enticing people to go for rides in their flying machines. Because they often used farmers' fields and paid farmers a small part of their proceeds, the activity became known as "barnstorming". Although, apart from one short jaunt in a Curtis JN–4, I had not been able to afford the luxury of flying, I had certainly developed the bug.

After Father returned from Europe, I heard how aviation had progressed during and since the First World War. I became increasingly fascinated with flying. I watched for hours as eagles and hawks glided high above our Fraser Valley farm, and imagined what it would be like to fly freely with them.

For years, I continued to read everything I could find relating to aviation. I knew flying would soon become a very important method of transporting goods and people. We were living in a vast country with great distances between most communities. Roads were unpaved and frequently not fit for travel. The aircraft was capable of rising above the deep mud and potholes, and cutting straight across the many switchbacks of those early highways. If aircraft was going to be the mode of transportation, it seemed wise for me to investigate the possibilities of becoming a pilot.

Since finishing my days at school, I had logged cottonwood while scrimping and saving every penny to eventually be able to fly. Now, at last, I had some money saved up and could finally join the Chilliwack Aero Club. The year was 1927. Membership was $25.00, still a lot of money in those days.

I took two hours of instruction, with Ginger Coote, in a "Golden Eagle" and was determined more than ever, flying would be my future. It would take me another seven years before I'd really be able to start flying. I'd have to save enough money to buy an aircraft of my own.

Russell L. (Ginger) Coote, 1900 – 1970, was the second son of Lt-Col. Andrew Coote, commanding officer of the 47th Battalion of the Canadian Expeditionary Force. Russel left Chilliwack in 1916 to join his father and his older brother Ian. He enlisted in his father's battalion as a bugler at twelve years of age and eventually fought in the trenches at fourteen. Towards the end of the war, Russel learned to fly with the Royal Flying Corp. and eventually the R.A.F. In 1920, he returned to Chilliwack where he sold the family farm to buy his first airoplane and soon began flying as a commercial aviator throughout British Columbia.

Among the pilots who flew for him were Rus Baker, Sheldon Luck and Margaret Rutledge. He also partnered with Grant McConachie. During the 1930s he began regular air service to the Gold Bridge and Zeballos gold fields.

Famous for his many mercy flights, it was reported by one newspaper that Ginger Coote had saved more lives than had been lost in all B.C. aviation accidents throughout the 1930's. At the outbreak of war in 1939, he sold his airline to serve as a volunteer with the Canadian Air Training Plan.

In all his 50 years as a pilot flying over some of the most challenging terrain in the world, Ginger Coote never damaged an "airoplane" and never lost a passenger.

As an added note, a collection of "extraordinary and scarce Canadian Expeditionary Force medals", having belonged to the three Coote W.W.I heroes, have been recently purchased from an auction in England by the Chilliwack Museum and Historical Society. (January, 2013).

It was a wild stab, but I asked Ginger to take my grandfather up for a ride. My grandfather went up, but when he came back down, he said: "If the Heavenly Father had wanted you to fly, He'd have given you wings. I think you'd better leave it."

I told my grandfather how I had once wanted to be a locomotive engineer, but my parents had discouraged the idea. This time I was determined to go through with becoming what I had dreamed of for so long. I wanted to be a pilot.

I had a couple of cows of my own on the homestead along with a few chickens. A large garden kept me supplied with vegetables. I could get deer from the hills and fish from the river. This permitted me to start saving money to pay for a private pilot's licence, the first step on the way to earning a commercial ticket, which would allow me to fly for hire. Despite the Depression, I still managed to save my money a dollar at a time.

THE AMERICAN EAGLE

In the spring of 1933, an American, Clarence Still, was flying a double winged *American Eagle*, powered by a Curtis OX-5 engine, from Bellingham up to Alaska. He had sold his plane to someone in Alaska and intended to deliver it in person. Since the machine was on floats he had decided to fly it up the coast. Clarence developed propeller trouble near Bella Coola, so he stopped there to order a new prop from the States.

While waiting for his prop, he began "barnstorming", that is flying passengers out of Bella Coola for money to help pay for his new propeller. Unfortunately for him, he had neglected to report to customs on his way into the country. He probably would have passed up the coast undetected had it not been for his barnstorming activities. The Provincial Police seized his aeroplane for the customs violation and brought it down to the Jericho Beach Air Force station in Vancouver, where it was put up for auction.

As soon as I heard about the auction, I went down and bid on the *American Eagle* and got that machine for three hundred dollars. That was the price owing on the new prop.

I managed to contact a pilot from Vancouver, by the name of Bill Lawson, to fly the plane up to Chilliwack for me the next day.

Bill and I checked the craft over quite carefully before putting her back into the water. Before long, we were air-born and heading for Chilliwack in my very own flying machine.

We came in on the river next to Father' s farm, where I pulled her up to the bank and tied her up securely.

The next step was to apply for registration papers. The Department of Transport gave me the letters: "CF-ATB". Then Carter Guest, a government aviation-inspector, came out and informed me I'd have to put new fabric on the wings. He also advised me to convert from floats to wheels. This meant I would have to build a runway. I spoke to Father about the runway and he thought that was a pretty good idea. I would have to take out some stumps that still cluttered up parts of his farm. Many were five feet in diameter or more.

During that summer, even though I didn't yet have a flying licence, I got a lot of taxi time on the river. It was my seaplane, and the Department of Transport personnel were in Vancouver. In other words, they were not there to catch me in the act. The exercise did teach me a lot about handling my aircraft on the water.

I think it would be hard for a layman to imagine the true difficulty of handling a craft of that vintage on a river. I would have to push the aeroplane far enough out into the stream and turn it around with the paddle so that it faced away from the shore. Then I would start the engine by hand, standing on the left float, behind the

58

propeller. By grasping a blade from behind I could swing it down briskly and, hopefully, the engine would catch. Of course if it did not, I would have to repeat the process. Sometimes the propeller would stop in a vertical position and it would be difficult to reach from the float - I'm short - but I always managed somehow.

During this time the current may have swung the seaplane to face the shore again and of course I'd have to resort to paddling to turn her around. Usually I got the engine started without much difficulty, then, I would have to walk back underneath the wing and climb into the cockpit.

The aircraft was not equipped with a water rudder. My only directional control was obtained by using the air rudder and of course this was not effective unless the engine was running fairly fast.

This led to quite a few tense moments, especially when getting close to shore. The lessons I learned on this machine in this fashion were probably some of the most valuable I ever received in handling an aircraft on the water.

As summer wore on, I became bolder and bolder. My confidence in handling the machine grew and I would taxi faster and faster. Of course, I would sometimes pass fairly close to various boats. This fun continued, until one afternoon, when I was charging down the river at high speed, I noticed the water surface had fallen away. Now, mother earth does not fall: I had taken off. When I realized this, I immediately reduced the power to idle. The aircraft settled back on to the water quite heavily. I was lucky nothing had been damaged. It was obvious I should finish my flying instruction before risking a total write-off. From then on, I was more careful, especially when taxiing at high speed.

As the leaves began to change colour, I built a long skid to put under the floats. Once the plane was positioned on the skid, I used a team of horses to pull the plane to the top of the riverbank. Every so often throughout the winter, chunks of ice would flow down from up river. If I left the aircraft in the water, the floats would have been damaged by ice. I contacted Clarence Still, the original owner. He agreed to sell me the wheels, landing-gear struts, and tailskid, which were still in his possession. He was happy to get some cash for the parts and glad to part with the memories of his dealings with Canada Customs.

During the previous summer, I had constructed a shed for the aeroplane. It would enable me to store the craft safely during the winter. The shed was only wide enough for the fuselage, main body of the aircraft and tailplanes (*horizontal stabilizer on the tail behind the main lifting surface*). Since I had to dismantle the craft to put new fabric on it, width would not be a problem.

I set the fuselage on the landing gear I'd bought from Clarence and removed the wings. I was able to push the fuselage into the shed and stand the wings on their leading edges, against the wall.

Next, I marked out an area on Dad's farm about 900 feet long and wide enough to qualify as a private runway.

All that fall and through the winter, I would walk down the three miles from my place on the island to Dad's farm and get the stump-puller going. The stump-puller was like a large cable jack. I would connect a cable between two large stumps, attach the stump-puller and start moving the lever back and forth to tighten the cable. I would then dig out around the roots of the stump I wanted to remove. Many times I would have to attach a longer lever to the stump-puller. The cable would get so tight I could put my weight on it without deflecting it. Eventually one of the stumps would start to come out of the ground. Some of the really big cottonwood stumps took several days to remove. If the weather was nice and there was enough light from the moon, I'd work until 10 or 11 o'clock at night.

That year, I managed to ship four or five booms from my homestead. With the money from the sale of the wood, I picked up an old Fordson tractor. I also borrowed a grader, one that had to be pulled with the tractor. With this equipment, I levelled out my runway and, by the following spring, had the 900 feet airstrip cleared and ready for business.

As winter rain soaked the runway, I set about repairing the aircraft. I took each wing into an old house that we were not using and proceeded to remove all the old fabric. I had an aircraft-maintenance engineer from Vancouver inspect the underlying structure. Then I performed all the necessary repairs and began to cover the wings with Irish linen. It took countless hours to hand-stitch the fabric to each wing.

I applied the first coat of clear nitrate dope and went home. Returning in the morning, I expected to see a nice tight fabric covering. Instead, it was all sagging down, limp, and totally useless. My heart sank. I was so discouraged, that instead of working on the aeroplane that day, I went out and continued clearing stumps, a great remedy for frustration.

Nitrate acts as a sealer for bare wood and uncoated covering materials strengthening and preparing the surface for paint.

When I returned in the evening to take a look, the fabric had tightened up somewhat. I decided to leave it for a couple of days before ripping it all off. I was soon to discover the high humidity had prevented the dope from drying properly. When it eventually did tighten up a bit, I applied another coat of dope.

In an effort to dry out the air in the hangar, I started heating the shed with a wood stove, while I was doping. The fumes got very strong. After one long session, I left the hangar and fell flat on my face as though I'd been drinking. It is a wonder that I had not blown myself up, as the fumes from dope are as volatile as gasoline fumes. Every time I threw more wood into the stove, I exposed the explosive atmosphere to an open flame. You wonder how I lived so long?

When the wings were completed, I recovered the fuselage and tailplane. The finish colour on the wings was orange and the fuselage was black. I finally moved the wings back into the shed and brought the engine into the house to start working on it.

Returning one morning after a particularly heavy snowfall, I found the shed partially collapsed about the aircraft. I figured for sure that this would be a major setback. When I entered the building to check on the damage, nothing had fallen on the machine itself. Some of the ceiling joists had broken in the middle and swung right down to the floor.

They had missed the fuselage, and did not crush the wings, which were leaning up against the wall. Relieved, I set about shoring up the building, so no more of the roof would collapse.

When the engine was dismantled, it proved to be in very good shape, requiring only rocker arm bushings, new piston rings and gaskets. Clifford Peene, an aircraft engineer, supervised the rebuilding process and signed off the work in the aircraft logbook.

By spring, I had the plane ready to fly and the runway was all finished. A young fellow by the name of Ronny Wells, whose parents owned a dairy farm in Sardis, came out to test-fly my plane. After the first test flight, he told me she was flying a little bit low on the left wing. I re-rigged the left wing by changing the angle-of-incidence.

> The angle-of-incidence is the angle at which the airfoil is inclined with respect to the centre of the fuselage.

Ronny took her up again and this time she was flying very well.

A few days later, Ronny took my *American Eagle* up for another flight. As he was landing, he "ground-looped", that is, he lost directional control on the ground. The plane swung around and took out a lower wing against one of my dad's plum trees. Not only did I have to rebuild the wing but Carter Guest, the aviation-inspector, insisted that I extend the runway to twelve hundred feet. Then my dad went out and cut down the plum tree. His regimental moustache was twitching and he sure appeared angry.

Many years later, I learned the old man had enjoyed every minute of the episode, chuckling all the time under his breath.

The destruction of the lower wing turned out to be a major setback for me. I had made arrangements with Clifford Peene, an air-engineer and flying instructor, to come out from Vancouver and fly the aircraft back. In Vancouver, he would teach me to fly. Now that the aircraft was damaged, this arrangement would fall through. The money I had saved up to pay him to teach me to fly would have to be used to repair the lower wing. That incident cost me one more year.

I moved the aeroplane back into the hangar and removed the damaged wing. Off came the brand-new fabric. I then created a jig on which to make new wing ribs. In between tooling new wing ribs, I removed all of the damaged ones from the spars. When I had made enough ribs to replace those that were damaged, I cleaned up the spars and slid the new ribs into place and secured them with glue and tiny nails. Everything was then given a couple of coats of varnish. Next, I stitched new Irish linen over the structure and applied the nitrate dope. This time, since it was summer, I did not have the sagging problem. There was less humidity to interfere with the drying process.

Since the repairs had diminished my savings account, I returned to my farm to clear more land and sell the logs for cash.

Lengthening the runway was much more work than I had calculated. Not only did I have massive stumps to remove, the only way I could get 1200 feet, was to angle the runway in a slightly different direction and fill in a ground depression. Filling in the depression was indeed a lot of extra work.

FROM HOMESTEADER TO PILOT

On February 1, 1936, I rented an apartment in Marpole, on the southern edge of Vancouver, and began flying lessons at the Vancouver Sea Island Air Base, with *The Foggin Flying Service*, for eight dollars an hour. Instruction was in a *Brunell Winkle Bird*. My teacher was Clifford Peene.

> *Leonard Foggin began flying at the old airport on Lulu Island in 1929, and became one of the first members of the Aero Club of B.C. In the spring of 1933, he purchased his first plane, a Kinner Bird BK biplane, which carried three people, the pilot in the rear with two passengers side by side in the front. Columbia Aviation would pay Len a commission for the use of his aircraft. In 1936, Len bought two more aeroplanes and Foggin Flying Service was born. Len qualified as a flying instructor in 1937 and devoted his full time to the company, hiring additional staff. Everyone who came to work for Len Foggin started in maintenance where they continued until they had acquired sufficient hours of flying time. Only then would they start to fly aircraft.*
>
> *The company grew and thrived with the addition of several planes until Len was killed in a flight accident On May 13, 1941.*

By February 24, I had logged eighteen hours and fifteen minutes. Then from March 4th to the 20th I flew another five hours. My old log book bears the simple notation, "Test; figure 8's, spins and four forced landings." Unlike today, the Department Of Transport Examiner stood on the ground to observe the student's performance. He did not sit in the aircraft where he could take control should I fail to recover from the spins. The figure 8's were performed over the centre line of the runway, and the instructor would be able to see if the turns were coordinated or not.

For the forced landings, I was instructed to fly over the field at a certain height and reduce the power to idle. Then, without touching the throttle, I was to bring the aircraft to a stop within a very small, designated area on the field.

With the successful completion of this test, and the written exams, I had earned my Private Pilot's Licence in a total of 25 hours and 35 minutes of airtime. I returned proudly home to Chilliwack on April 25th, 1936.

Pushing my own *American Eagle* out of its hangar, I checked her over carefully. Having done most of the rebuilding work myself, I felt very comfortable. Now it was time to reap the reward from all the labour.

With the fuel tank topped up and plenty of oil on the dipstick, I gave each rocker arm a squirt of fresh oil and closed the engine cowlings. I set chalks in front of the wheels, and pulled the propeller through a few revolutions to prime the engine. My father had offered to start the engine so I got in and when everything was ready, I leaned over to one side so I could speak clearly to him. I switched on the magneto and hollered "Contact!" The engine barked and soon settled down to a smooth idle as Dad stepped out of the way. When I gave the signal he walked in along the leading edge of the lower wing to pull the chalk away from each wheel. With a wave, and a grin that stretched from ear to ear, I taxied out to my own airstrip.

When the engine had warmed up, there was nothing left to do except takeoff. The *American Eagle* lifted off easily from the 1200 feet of sod runway.

The magneto is an electrical generator, used to provide power to the engine.

I spent the better part of an hour flying around the Chilliwack area, before returning to the farm. My runway appeared so small from the air compared to the large landing field on Sea Island. I wondered how I could land on it and stop before the end. However, I knew I had to give it a try.

On the final approach, I purposely came down low over the river. Just off the end of the runway, I was actually a little below the river bank and had to pull up to get onto the airstrip. This bled off quite a bit of speed and the aircraft plopped down without bouncing. I held the stick all the way back, trying to apply as much pressure to the tail skid as possible, since this was the only brake on the aircraft. I had visions of my plane running off the end of the short strip into the stumps and destroying what had taken so much painstaking labour to rebuild. The aircraft rumbled to a stop, and as the adrenaline drained from my veins, I was able to observe about three quarters of the runway still out in front of the aircraft. I was relieved. I also realized at that point I would not have to go to such extreme measures to land at home.

On that first day, I made three flights. Throughout the summer, on any day that was good for flying, I would walk down from my place on the Island to Dad's farm and fly. The goal was to obtain enough airtime to qualify for the Commercial Pilot's Licence. Then, I would be able to fly for a living. Quite a few times, the front seat would be occupied by family members or by any friend who happened by at the time. Late one afternoon, Carter Guest stopped by and suggested I move over to Earl Bretts' runway, about seven miles away. It was a much longer runway and Carter Guest thought it would be safer to operate from.

So I flew out of Brett's field for part of that summer. Although it was a larger strip, with more open fields around, it was a much further walk from my island.

Roy Brett was very involved in aviation, and encouraged anyone interested to pursue a career in flying. He also spent time helping and encouraging Aero clubs to become established in communities along the Coast and on Vancouver Island. It was through his efforts and the efforts of the people he encouraged that many of the communities in British Columbia have an airstrip today.

> Roy Brett went missing November 15, 1970, on a flight from Powell River to Chilliwack. The wreckage was found 37 years later in Mission, B.C.

Flying out of Roy's field was not without its incidents. The OX-5 engine that powered the *American Eagle* had only one magneto. If the points on that one magneto pitted or failed, because the condenser was no longer any good, the engine would stall. One time, I was doing circuits out of Roy's field when the engine failed. Since I was fairly close to the runway, I elected to make my forced landing but lost a bit more height in the turn than I'd hoped for. As I crossed the fence on the approach end of the runway, the tailskid of my aeroplane struck the top rail. I landed on the runway without further incident and, to my surprise, my tailskid was still intact. It did not take long to find the cause of the engine failure and repair it.

> Tailskids are the rear landing point, replaced by wheels on more modern aircraft.

On another occasion, the engine stopped when I was a little further from the runway, and I was forced to land in a farmer's field. Of course the aircraft left a trail of damaged hay. I went over to the farmhouse and offered to pay the farmer for the amount of crop damage. He was not worried about the small amount of

68

hay I had mowed. His first concern was that I was all right.

When I had assured him that neither I, nor the aircraft, had suffered any harm, he offered to help in anyway he could. I told him that we could repair the engine where the aircraft stood and probably turn around and takeoff in the same track in which I had landed, thereby keeping the damage to his crop at a minimum. The farmer was very happy with this. In return for his generosity, I offered to give him a ride out of Roy's field once I returned there. Although he was pleased I made the offer, he never did take me up on it.

Some people I took up for rides became very excited. It was quite an accomplishment in those days to travel along at 90 mph., especially since the fastest they had probably ever been in a car on the old dirt roads was perhaps 35 to 40 mph. One such person was my sister Kay. She was visibly excited as she climbed up on the wing to get into the front cockpit. She stepped over the cockpit side directly onto the seat and then lowered herself into the aircraft, stretching her feet out in front of her as she sat down. I helped her put on the seat belt and handed her a pair of flying goggles.

The two cockpits are open to the elements.

We took off and flew around the Fraser Valley. My sister pointed out various sights she recognized and flashed me big smiles. It was obvious she was talking and describing some things but it was not possible to hear her over the roar of the V8 engine. It was a great feeling to be able to make my younger sister so happy.

All was going quite well until I returned to Roy Brett's field and joined the circuit. When I turned on to the crosswind leg, it meant we were flying straight at the mountain that towered above the airstrip to the South. Kay undid her seatbelt and stood up in the seat, in front of me. She pointed at the mountain and was talking a mile-a-minute. It was obvious to me she was concerned we were about to crash into its immense bulk, but I was horrified that the slightest bit of turbulence could knock her out of the cockpit causing her to fall from the aircraft.

Of course, her chances of surviving in such a catastrophe would not have been very good. I motioned for her to sit down, but all she could do was turn and look at the mountain and turn back to me with a worried look on her face. I entered the turn to the final approach very carefully, so as not to knock my sister off-balance. Only when the mountain was no longer in front of the aeroplane, did she sit down.

We landed without any further excitement. Kay was so elated. I tried to point out to her the risk she had taken by standing up, but all she could understand was that she had prevented me from crashing into the mountain, by pointing it out for me. Of course she remembered that flight for the rest of her life.

Throughout 1936, I gave quite a few people rides in my flying machine, trying to build time for my commercial licence. Not only did I receive pleasure from the actual flying, but also from the enjoyment the rides gave to my various passengers. Inspired by this realization, I flew down to Barnston Island on the day after Christmas in 1936, and over the next few days, gave free rides to the local children.

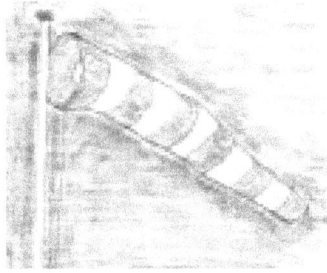

THE WIND

Sometimes the wind can suddenly change direction. The aeroplane then has to be flown at a crab angle, with the nose pointing at an angle of 10 or 15 degrees off a straight line. This can be especially dangerous during taking off or landing when the ditch at the side of the runway is waiting to swallow you up. Even if you do get up into the air, the wind will try to push you off course. It takes skill and determination to overcome crosswind and fly right.

While flying cross-country, the wind can change direction and come at you from behind. Sudden turbulence or down drafts can even flip a plane over, if the pilot is not prepared and vigilant.

On a calm day, flying is a breeze. The aircraft is not knocked around in turbulence. The pilot can relax and enjoy the ride. On a windy day, however, the aeroplane seems eager to get into the air and ascent can be swift. Wind or no wind, the pilot finds joy in knowing he's accomplishing what men had wanted to do ever since they watched eagles gliding above the hills. Man is flying!

For a while, I was staying with a friend from New Westminster. This gave me a chance to visit the city and spend a night on the town. My friend had arranged for the use of a farmer's field on Barnston Island for a landing strip. The island is situated a few miles up the Fraser River from New Westminster. My friend drove out to pick me up in his car, a *Durant*, I believe.

The field proved to be quite suitable for landing, and there was plenty of room for takeoff. The fall rains had not yet made the field too soft to use as an airfield. I pulled the plane nose up to the side of the barn and secured it as well as I could, by driving a few stakes into the ground and tying the wings and tail to them. Once I was satisfied my craft was secure, we headed for the city.

Upon returning the next day I was happy to see that the plane was where I had secured it, but my heart sank as we got closer. Fabric was hanging in tatters from the elevators, which were bent totally out of shape.

Elevators are the movable flaps on the wings that change the shape of the trailing edge of the wing, allowing the aeroplane to land slower and not use as much runway.

The farmer came out to explain that he had let his horse out and that he had no idea that the horse would bother the aircraft. The creature had been amusing himself for some time by stepping on the trailing edge of the elevators and letting his foot slide off. This would cause the elevators to spring up and bounce a bit. The horse had kept this up until the farmer saw what he was doing and ran out to put a stop to it.

It would not be possible to fly the craft in this condition. The only thing I could do was to remove the damaged elevators and take them out to a repair shop at the Vancouver airport on Sea Island. I borrowed some tools from the farmer and kept my mutterings that the horse would probably benefit from a one-way ride to the glue factory, to myself, as I removed the elevators. I put the damaged parts in the back of my friend's car, and we drove out to the shop at Sea Island. The mechanic in the shop welded in some new steel tubing to replace the material that had been damaged.

After getting the structure repaired, I returned home to Chilliwack with the elevator. There I re-covered the damaged section with Irish linen. It took a fair amount of work to complete. The fabric had to be stitched onto the frame and given a couple of coats of clear dope. Then it had to be sewn to the ribs about every four inches. When the fabric was secured tightly to the frame, I glued narrow strips of fabric over top of the stitches with more dope. Over this, I applied a couple of coats of aluminium (silver) dope before applying the final colour.

Just about 2 1/2 months later, in the middle of March 1937, I made my way back to Barnston Island with my repaired elevator, which I spent the morning installing on the aircraft. You can be sure I checked the rest of the aircraft over very carefully just in case that darned horse had been near it again.

Untying the *American Eagle*, I pushed back from the barn and turned my aeroplane around to face out into the field. I lifted the cowlings and used a pump type oilcan to squirt oil on all 16 valve guides and on the rocker arms. When the cowlings were secured, I primed the Curtis OX-5 engine and pulled the propeller through a few times. I spent a little time showing the farmer the proper method of swinging the propeller to start the engine. When I was satisfied he knew what to do and that he would not be in danger of injury, I climbed in and did up my seat belt. I held the stick full back, cracked the throttle forward about a quarter inch, switched on the single magneto and signalled to the farmer.

With a brisk motion, the farmer pulled down on the propeller and swung it through. White puffs of smoke belched from the exhaust stacks on each side of the cowling as the engine barked to life. The plane shook a little bit and then settled into a smooth idle. I made sure the farmer had made his way clear of the aircraft, while I waited for the water temperature to rise sufficiently.

Once the engine was warm enough, I gave it a little blast of throttle, while holding a little forward stick to help lift the tailskid and get the aircraft moving.

I lined up into the wind, turned and waved goodbye to the farmer and eased the throttle all the way forward. The engine speed increased to between 1500 to 1600 rpm, giving me 90 horsepower. After a run of less than about 400 feet, the *American Eagle* became light on the wheels. Gentle backpressure on the stick eased her into the air.

It felt good to have my baby operational again, even though she had only been unserviceable for two-and-a-half months. It had seemed a part of me had been missing during all that time.

MORE UPS AND DOWNS

During 1937, I did not manage to get as much flying time into the logbook as I'd hoped. There was a tremendous amount of work to do on the new farm. The only method of gaining extra cash was to cut more hardwood for sale.

By November 1937 I had managed to put in the required number of flying hours for a Commercial Pilot's Licence. November 4th, I took the flight test and, at last, obtained my goal. By that time, however, I realized a fresh commercial licence would not be enough to secure a flying job. The commercial operators were looking for people with closer to a thousand hours of flying experience. It became clear to me that the only way I was going to get that amount of airtime, would be to become an instructor myself. This also meant I would have to continue logging and river towing.

During the following year, I also set up a small logging camp near Chihalis. If all went as planned, I would be able to get enough money put away to pay for enough construction on the new camp to be able to afford to become a flying instructor within about a year.

I still flew the *American Eagle* periodically. Very often I would drop in on Roy Brett's field. I enjoyed going there because the field had much more room and better approaches than I had on my private airstrip on Dad's farm.

I received word from the small logging camp in Chihalis they were short of a few supplies. It would be a fairly long trip up in the boat, but only about twenty minutes each way in the aeroplane. There was no place to land the *American Eagle* near Chihalis, since my plane was on wheels. I got the bright idea that if I made a parachute, it would be possible to drop the bundle into the camp. I scrounged around for some old material and twine, bundled up all the articles in a sack, attached the parachute, and took it out to the *Eagle*.

I made sure there would be enough room to carry it without interfering with the control-column while I was flying and that it would be easy to toss the load over the side.

Having seen to all these preparations, I took off and flew up to the camp. I made a low pass to get someone's attention and on the next pass, tossed the bundle out of the open cockpit in such a fashion that it would miss the tail of the aircraft. The makeshift parachute opened, and the supplies landed close enough to camp for everyone to be happy. I rocked my wings and turned towards home.

Not long after that, I noticed the engine was starting to get hot. It was evident I was losing water from either the radiator or one of the radiator hoses. There were no places to land between where I was and home, so I pressed on, hoping the engine would not seize before I could land safely. That was another of those longest ten minutes I ever spent. Finally my airstrip came into view. The engine was boiling by that time and no longer producing full power because it was so hot. I sat there hoping against all hope it would get me the rest of the way home. It seemed to take so much longer to cover the distance now that the engine was failing.

Finally, after what seemed like hours, I knew I could land on the airfield and started a straight-in approach. Over the lowered nose of the aircraft, right between the cabane struts, (*cabane struts on a biplane support the upper wing over the fuselage.*) I could see Dad's horse munching grass right in the middle of the runway. Had it been on any other day it would have been a simple matter to fly low over the field and chase him off, but there was no way I could stay in the air any longer. I landed straight ahead expecting to plow into the horse. I guess the animal was alerted by the sound of my landing. As I came in, he raised his head, looked at the aeroplane, and nonchalantly sauntered out of the way.

When I had reduced the throttle to idle, the propeller came to an abrupt stop. Once I had rolled to a complete halt, I got out and tried to move the propeller by hand. It would not budge. I left the machine where it was, figuring I had damaged the engine.

The next day I returned to put the plane in the hangar and discovered the propeller would move, so I started it up. It ran as though nothing had ever happened to it. In fact the engine ran quite well for a few more years before the *American Eagle* was finally retired.

TEACHING FOR THE AIR FORCE

At long last, towards the end of the summer of 1939, I qualified to become an instructor. I was hired by the Foggin Flying Service, to teach young men to fly so as to enable them to qualify for the Royal Canadian Air Force. When the Second World War began, I was giving initial instruction on aircraft like the *Fleet Canuck* and the *Luscome.*

Radios were fairly primitive in those days, so very often we depended on a system of coloured lights, observed from the Control-Tower, to give us our clearances for movement about the airport and for taking-off and for landing. I was flying from around nine o'clock almost every morning until sunset. This built up my time fairly rapidly so that, within my first year of starting, I had logged well over fifteen hundred hours. Ironically, at 36 and having a wife and children, I myself was considered too old for the Air Force.

My most exceptional student soloed in four hours. Of course Len Foggin was not too happy because he would not receive as much money for this person's basic training as for the rest of the students. I found myself in the position of having to defend myself and explained that the young man had caught on very quickly and, in my opinion, it seemed pointless to put him through more hours practicing takeoff's and landings just to build up more time before he went solo. I figured he was as ready as he'd ever be and pilots were desperately needed for overseas service.

There is a special relationship between the primary instructor and the student. The first instructor introduces the would-be pilot to the realm of flight and gives him the basic skills with which to control an aircraft. For the instructor it is not unlike a parent raising a child and taking delight in the infant's first steps. The act of sending a student on his first solo flight, gives the new flyer the realization that no longer is he condemned to crawl about the surface of the earth. Instead, he now has the ability to soar above the clouds. At that point, the student also realizes there is still much to learn, but the instructor has trained him or her to master the basics and be ready to learn through the school of experience.

I had been an instructor for Foggin's Flying Service long enough that I would later meet up with some of my first students who had survived flying with the Royal Canadian Air Force as well as the British RAF.

Of course they were happy to relate some of the experiences they had in the war. Some of the aircraft they flew were quite exciting: swift fighters like the *Hawker Hurricane* and *Spitfire*. Some flew large bombers. The conditions they operated under were very bad in some cases, but the exuberance of the young men could make up for almost anything.

During the sessions with these flyers, I could see the tremendous change the war had brought upon them. At first I would inquire about other students I had instructed at the same time as these fellows. Very often the answer was that their friends had been maimed or killed overseas. Such had been the fate of the student who had soloed in four hours. According to his friends, he died in North Africa.

The realities of war were difficult to accept at times. At first I was happy to meet up with past students returning from the front. Later, I found it easier to listen to their stories while resisting the urge to inquire about their buddies who had trained along with them.

I am sure it was much more difficult for the parents and families of those young men who had given so much during those years.

CANADIAN AIRWAYS

By 1940 I had enough flying time to upgrade my commercial ticket to a Public Transport Licence. I talked to a fellow by the name of Walter Gilbert, from *Canadian Airways* who suggested I apply to fly for them. When my application was accepted, I gave notice to Len Foggin.

I was soon flying for *Canadian Airways*, owned by James Richardson, out of Winnipeg, and co-founded by Walter Gilbert and James Richardson. Of course Len was not happy about losing me, but I saw no future in remaining as a flying instructor. Len would have no trouble finding a replacement.

The pilots and engineers at *Canadian Airways* had difficulty remembering my first name, Ayliffe. Before long, they were all calling me "Pat", many of them being under the impression I was Irish. Pat has stuck with me to this day.

I made a few trips flying a *Waco* up the West Coast. This was one of the cabin models, powered by a Jacobs engine, and of course it was on floats. One of those trips took me back to Port Mellon where I had worked for a while trying to save money for flying lessons. Naturally, I had to drop in to visit my former employer. My old boss said he had watched for me to return with my boat for quite a few weeks before he gave up.

Of course, he had no way of knowing I had done what I'd said I'd do, until I dropped in on him with the *Waco*. He was glad I had come by because, from time to time, he had wondered what had become of me over the past few years. He was happy to see I had been successful and we parted on good terms.

Next, I was sent to fly containers of gasoline into Buttle Lake, west of Campbell River. At that time the lake was inaccessible except by air. When the work at Campbell River was finished, Spring had come and the company needed a pilot back at Lac du Bonnet , Manitoba. I drove all the way in my car, a *Hudson Terraplane*. When I arrived at the base, Bill Catton, Winnipeg superintendent for *Canadian Airways*, checked me out in a *Junkers W 34*, in the twin-engine *Dragon Rapide*, and in a *Norseman*.

For my first trip, Bill sent me off to Berrens River and on to Favourable Lake, Ontario. I had become so accustomed to flying mountain valleys that I felt lost over the flat terrain of the prairies and spent most of the time identifying each little lake on the map as I progressed to my first destination. It felt like I was on my first cross-country flight all over again. I completed the trip without a problem, but it took a few weeks to become comfortable navigating without the mountains I had become so familiar with. I spent the whole summer flying out of Lac du Bonnet. Most of the time was spent on the Berrens River mail run.

Towards the end of summer, I was given the task of freighting some strange looking machinery into a small Lake just north of Lac du Bonnet. Two brothers were assembling what appeared to be a small combine, on the front-end of a scow. At first they were reluctant to explain what they were doing, because they didn't want any competition. When I had gained their confidence, they told me they were going to use the equipment to harvest the wild rice growing in the lake. I understand they continued to harvest that rice for many years in what proved to be a very profitable venture.

The business is still thriving with over 170,000 lbs. of wild rice being processed in Lac du Bonnet and sold to markets in Canada and Europe (recorded in 1997).

Early one morning, *Canadian Airways* sent me to Winnipeg to pick up a *Gullwing Stinson*. The plane wasn't ready until late the following afternoon so, when I finally got the O.K. to go, I was quite anxious to leave. I performed my standard pre-flight check, pumped the residual water out of the floats and got ready to take off. No one had told me there were children swimming in the Red River.

I was on the step, coming around the bend in the river, and almost air-born, when I noticed children in the water.

It was too late to stop and impossible to turn to avoid them, so with my right hand pressing the throttle against the firewall, I eased the control column back and luckily cleared the water before getting to where the youngsters were. Children could have been hurt or drowned. I imagine it was quite a site for them to see an aircraft fly barely a foot above their heads. The thought of what would have happened, had I been heavily loaded, filled me with dread.

Mr. Woods was the base manager at Lac du Bonnet and he noticed I was looking quite pale. He asked me if anything had happened. I told him about the near miss with the children. He told me no one had contacted him about it and fortunately, nothing ever came of the incident. If I had nightmares, they were of children drowning in the wake of my aircraft. On occasion, birds have flown into my windshield. The thought of running into a fellow human being, especially a child, was terrifying.

For quite a while my job involved flying the *Gullwing Stinson* and management had put in what they called "an oil-dilution system" developed by Tommy Siers, one of the engineers in Winnipeg. Multi-grade oils had not yet been developed. In the temperatures aircraft are subjected to every winter in this country, the single-grade aviation oil we used often became more like tar. It would become impossible for the oil pump to move cold oil through small engine passages. Every pilot knew that if an engine was started without first being warmed and filled with pre-warmed oil, the aircraft engine would simply be destroyed. Tommy came up with the idea that, if oil was premixed with gasoline, sufficient for the prevailing temperature, the oil would then be able to be pumped through the engine passages even at the coldest temperatures experienced in the Arctic. Tommy Siers also believed that, once the oil came up to the operating temperature of the engine, the gasoline would boil off.

The gasoline-vapor would then be exhausted harmlessly through the engine breather. This would leave the pure oil to perform its job of lubricating the engine for the rest of the day.

Of course the following procedure would have to be repeated anytime the engine was to be shut down long enough to cool right off to the local temperature. After landing, we had to wait until the engine temperature went down to about forty degrees, then we restarted the engine. I would then hold a spring-loaded switch in the "on" position for a predetermined period of time. This opened a solenoid valve to mix gasoline with the engine lubricating oil as it returned to the oil tank. The longer I idled the engine with this switch activated, the more gasoline was mixed with the engine lubricating oil. I was instructed to time the short engine run for about three minutes.

During the testing period, I had to write out reports on every flight, including the temperature outside. For about a month, I reported on everything concerning that engine, the number of hours flown and so on. Since those tests were being conducted towards the end of Summer, the engineer did not have to drain the oil after the day's flying, however it did create some other work for him.

This research was conducted before detergent oils were widely in use. The gasoline in the oil tended to act like a super cleaner and loosen the accumulated carbon in the engine. The carbon would then collect in the oil screen. If the engineer did not clean the oil screen following every few hours of operation, the carbon would plug the screen and starve the engine of oil. Of course there would be only so much carbon in the engine, so after a few times, there would be less and less in the oil screen. Then the engineer could return to the standard inspection intervals.

Following a couple of months of operating this test, the company took the plane back to Winnipeg and sent the engine out for overhaul. Since this engine had been used for testing purposes, special attention was paid to the dimension of all of the parts. The inspectors found there was almost no abnormal wear on that engine. That was only part of the research on oil-dilution on aircraft engines. Many other pilots contributed information in this manner on other systems and other engines.

That fall, *Canadian Airways* needed a pilot back in Vancouver. I was picked to return to flying on the B.C.

Coast. On the way back I was to deliver a *Fairchild 71* to Russ Baker in Fort St. James.

> *Russel (Russ) Baker began as a barnstormer in Manitoba before becoming a bush pilot with a reputation for mercy flights. He flew for Canadian Airways, then for C.P. Air, which, at that time, belonged to the Canadian Pacific Railway Company.*
>
> *In 1946, Russ founded Central B.C. Airlines as a charter outfit out of Fort St. James, in Northern B.C. The new company absorbed smaller airlines, expanding to Alberta and Saskatchewan. In 1957, Central B.C. Airlines became Pacific Western Airlines. P.W.A. flew over the Pole to London and later to the Orient.*

I would later be offered an Orient route but, by that time, I preferred the bush flying – which I loved better than any other type of flying.

The *Fairchild 71* I delivered to Russ Baker, had been used in making the film, *Captains of the Clouds* starring, if I remember right, James Cagney, Dennis Morgan and Brenda Marshall. A *Canadian Airways* agent from Berrens River, by the name of Burt Reilly, decided to accompany me on the trip to Vancouver because he wanted to see what the West Coast was like.

We departed from Winnipeg and crossed Lake Winnipeg en route to The Pas. Landing at The Pas late that afternoon, we filled the gas tanks and topped up the oil. It was too late to proceed any further so we stayed the night.

We were up early the next morning and got away in good time. I was bucking quite a strong headwind and by the time we got to Edmonton, was running low on fuel, so I decided to drop down on Cooking Lake. We fuelled up fairly quickly and took off. The headwind was still very strong and by the time we got to Jasper, we had used a lot of fuel for the distance travelled. I landed on Moose Lake at the head of the Fraser River and walked about half a mile into Redpass Junction, where I managed to obtain a barrel of aviation fuel. The only way to get that barrel of gasoline to the aeroplane was to roll it down the railroad tracks for three or four hundred yards and then down to the lakeshore where the aircraft was docked. That took quite a while, but I finally got there and pumped the contents of the barrel into the aircraft.

It was fairly late in the afternoon, by the time we departed. I followed the Fraser River down to a place called Penney. Since it was getting late and the cloud base was fairly low, I decided to remain there overnight.

By the following morning the weather had improved somewhat. We continued on to Prince George, where we stopped again for fuel and then headed for Stewart Lake. When we arrived, we were asked to wait for the arrival of Russ Baker so I could take the *Dragon Rapide* he was flying on to Vancouver. Russ arrived, and I turned the *Fairchild 71* over to him, also passing on the film history of the aircraft. By the time I arrived in Vancouver with the *Dragon Rapide*, I was convinced she needed some tender loving care. Vancouver dispatch wanted me to depart for the West coast of Vancouver Island right away. I asked them to have several of the maintenance staff look over the aircraft and attend to a few items first.

Late that afternoon I took off and managed to get as far as Port Alberni, where I had to stay overnight. The next morning I continued on to the North end of the Island to pick up passengers for Vancouver.

During that same year, I would sometimes fly passengers down the West Coast of Vancouver Island, which, quite often, could be covered in fog and subject to high winds. On one trip, the weather was so bad I had to put into Zeballos and stay at the local hotel with my passenger. He didn't seem to mind the delay, as he brought out a bottle of Scotch and we proceeded to have a few drinks. Not having had much experience with drinking, I thought everything was fine, until I got up out of my chair. The world was spinning round and walls and floor kept shifting. I knew I would have to go down to the restaurant and get something to eat. The next thing I knew, I went flying head-over-heels down the stairs. Mr. Blackburn, the manager of the hotel looked at me and laughed. "What have you been up to, Pat?"

He made sure I wasn't hurt before he took me in for some coffee. A little later, I ate a good supper and went early to bed. The following morning I felt fine, except for a few bruises. We flew into Tofino and then on to Vancouver.

Most of the passenger transport out of Vancouver involved flying the twin-engine *Dragon Rapide*. I had been with this aircraft for a couple weeks when I was switched to the *Norseman*, a single engine plane. My first trip in the *Norseman* was up to Port Alice and back. It happened to be a good day, so the flying was easy, so easy in fact that I allowed my mind to wander extensively. About ten miles out of Vancouver on my return, a broad grin spread across my face. I was about to have some fun. I tuned the radio to the company dispatch frequency, picked up the microphone and held it close my lips.

"Vancouver dispatch, Vancouver dispatch, this is Pat Carey returning on one engine." I said, with a touch of urgency in my voice.

Vancouver dispatch fell for my joke hook, line, and sinker. They replied "What is your position? What's your altitude? Can you make it down OK?"

I was having a good laugh and to make it even better, the radio reception was exceptionally good that day, for the lady who was the radio operator in Port Alice had heard the whole thing. She simply pressed her mike button and laughed. This alerted Vancouver dispatch that they had fallen for one of my little pranks. Of course the dispatcher gave me the cold shoulder for a short time after my return and that made me grin even more.

I flew out of Vancouver all that winter. The following spring of 1942, the company sent me up to Prince George with the *Fairchild 82*. Soon after my arrival, I was flying the *Junkers W34* on floats. I did a lot of flying for a group of engineers who were up from the United States. They were known as the *Rocky Mountain Engineers*, attached to the American military. The Engineers were surveying the Rocky Mountain trench to check the feasibility of building a railroad from Prince George through to Alaska. I was kept fairly busy just supplying their camps and moving personnel to each progressive site.

One time during that summer, I had been particularly busy. I returned late one afternoon and the aircraft was due for an inspection and maintenance. The engineer, Ed Hanratty, offered to work late into the night, so I might resume flying early the next day. Since he would be working most of the night I agreed to service the aircraft in the morning with fuel and oil and depart on my first trip without his assistance.

The next morning, while I was gassing up the *Junkers*, a fellow came up to me and stated he had permission to accompany me on that day's flight.

He just told me his name but didn't say whom or what he represented. He handed me a slip of paper much like a ticket, which I put in my pocket. I returned to the business of getting the aircraft ready. By that time, it had become my habit to wear work clothes and sometimes coveralls. It did not make a lot of sense to wear a white shirt and tie, when most of the time on the ground was spent loading and unloading all kinds of freight.

I was topping up the oil tank, when this fellow looked at me and asked, "Where's the pilot?" Now this innocent question wasn't the best one to ask of a pilot in those days. We usually seized on the chance to tease any hapless passenger who looked like he might have a fairly good sense of humour. My mark for the day had just arrived so I replied "Oh, that guy. He's the laziest bum I've ever known in the whole world, he's never out of bed this early in the morning. You're not going to fly with him are you?"

To top it off, I added, "Besides I think he's goofy!"

"Well, I'm supposed to go on this trip," he replied. I finished wiping the morning dew off the windshields, getting them good and clean; then I said: " Okay, jump in."

He hesitated, "I'm not going to fly with you."

"Don't worry, he should be along any minute now; you may as well climb up into the right hand seat and wait for him."

As soon as he was far enough into the aircraft, I undid the mooring line and pushed the plane out into the river.

"Where's the pilot?" my passenger asked.

"Well," I said, "I'm not waiting for that darned pilot any longer. I've waited long enough. It's time to go, so we are going."

The young man looked very nervous as he reached for his seat belt, and he watched me closely. He watched everything I did with great interest, as I taxied up river towards the bridge and took off.

After a while, it dawned on him I was the pilot and that he'd made a mistake thinking I was the engineer. He had a good laugh about the trick I had played on him. I noticed he made some notes throughout the flight. He didn't say much more even though we didn't return until late that evening. He seemed to be quite happy with the experience and thanked me for the trip, as he departed.

A couple of mornings later, a base engineer by the name of Gordon Scott, who was working for *Pan American Airlines*, came up to me and said: "Look here – look at what's in the paper."

Well, it turned out that this fellow was a reporter for the Vancouver Sun and he wrote everything that had happened and how he had thought I was the engineer. All the people in Prince George who knew me sure got a kick out of that.

As the summer progressed, the survey party got very close to Fort Ware. One morning, two officers from the United States military arrived in Prince George and I was instructed to take them up to survey the progress the men in the camps were making. They were quite pleased with the results being produced, and since they had come such a great distance, when their work was finished, they decided to become tourists at Fort Ware.

The area west of Hudson Hope is now flooded by Williston Lake, from MacKenzie at the south end, almost as far north as Fort Ware.

For the return trip we picked up a couple of extra passengers: one of the officers from the survey camp, and a trapper by the name of Del Miller. When I reached cruising altitude, I glanced around to see how everyone was doing and was surprised to see all four men seated in the circle on the cabin floor. They were playing some sort of dice game. Herb, my brother, happened to be the mechanic assigned to assist me on this trip. I was curious to see what was going on, so I said to Herb, "You take over for a while, I'm going back to see what's going on."

He had been on enough trips with me by that time that he could fly the aircraft straight and level. He could not yet take off or land. As I left my seat and ducked through the small door to the cabin, I instructed Herb to simply follow the river that stretched out ahead of us.

I stood in the front of the cabin and watched the game proceed. It was obvious money was being wagered. Someone would roll the dice and, depending on what was scored, the winner would pick the cash up from the floor. The players were fairly engrossed in their game but after a little while, Del looked up at me and asked: "Pat, who's flying the aeroplane?"

"Oh, my brother Herb" I replied.

"I didn't know he could fly" replied Del.

"No, neither did I until just now."

Well, I tell you that broke up the dice game right then and there. They absolutely refused to play any further until I returned to the pilot seat. Since it was pointless to stay while they just sat on the floor watching me, I returned to the cockpit and resumed control. The dice game resumed.

As we continued, the turbulence became worse. I turned around and told them through the open doorway they should return to their seats because the ride was about to get rougher. They waved to indicate they had heard me, however, they continued their game. Then we hit a really bad bump, and everything that was loose went to the roof of the aircraft. I looked around and there were four men in sitting position just floating more than a foot above the floor. That sure put a stop a to the dice game. They scrambled into their seats and did up their seat belts.

The U.S. Engineers made steady progress that summer. Because there were very few lakes suitable for even the smallest aircraft in the area just north of Fort Ware, and since the Engineers were going on to Fort

Liard and Watson Lake, they got a fellow by the name of Skooke Davidson to run a pack-train up there for them. I had to fly a load of supplies into Mud River where Skooke had his base camp. I got in there and unloaded. I felt uneasy all the time we had been unloading because there had not been very much room for landing.

As I taxied out into the river, my mouth was dry. There was not a lot of room from where I could start the take off run to the next bend in the river. I swung the aircraft around and throttled up to full power, knowing I had to get it up on the step quickly and off the water as soon as possible. We cleared the trees at the next bend in the river with almost no room to spare. I really didn't want to fly back in there.

It was getting late in the evening, so we stopped at a small lake called Fox Lake. We'd had no lunch and no supper, but I said to the engineer, Ed Hanratty, that we'd better stay there the night, as I didn't want to land on the river at Fort Ware after dark. We put our backs underneath the tail of the aircraft and pushed it up the sandy beach until the tail end of the floats rested hard on the shore. Even though the aircraft was secured very well in this fashion, we still attached a rope from one of the back bollards on a float, to a small tree on the bank. We put our sleeping bags out on the sand and went to sleep pretty quickly. In the morning we saw the tracks where a moose had stepped over both our sleeping bags during the night. Neither of us had heard a thing. We shuddered to think what the scenario might have been had wolves been chasing the moose.

That fall, the engineers completed their work in the Rocky Mountain Trench and I was sent back to Fort St. James.

A new mine had started up, north of Fort St. James. Because of the mine's location, everything had to be flown in. I ended up doing a lot of freighting for them.

In the spring of '43, I had the privilege of flying out the first bottles of mercury from this mine called *Tackla Mercury*. They actually extracted the mercury from the ore at the mine site. From then on, when I flew supplies in, I would end up bringing out about five bottles of mercury weighing fifty pounds each. We would support the bottles in a specially constructed wood box and tie them down tight. If those bottles ever got loose in turbulence, they would do a lot of damage to the aircraft. If the mercury spilled, it would flow into the lower seams of the aircraft, where it would be impossible to reclaim and would cause the aluminium to corrode rapidly.

WOLVES

That fall, we were just getting in the last of the trips to *Tackla Mercury* before the changeover from floats to skis. The office manager came to me and said "I have a load that has to go out today."

It was rather late in the day and I told him I didn't like the look of the weather. However, he insisted the load had to go out right away. So I finally agreed to go. The pilot has the final say, but you have to listen to the customer.

Other than pushing poor weather, the trip into the mine was uneventful. I off-loaded the aircraft and took off on the return leg to Fort St. James as quickly as possible.

On the return trip I could see the weather was deteriorating. To make matters worse, darkness would come early with the extra heavy cloud cover. Within moments of my takeoff, rain and drizzle turned into snow and visibility dropped to almost zero. I was right down close to the trees which were getting harder and harder to see because of the snow on them. Suddenly, I came across a dark patch. The darkness extended quite a distance and I realized it was a lake. Knowing how much room I had from the amount of time that had passed since entering the patch, I immediately swung around and landed on the reverse course.

I finally got the aircraft into a little spit, out of the wind and turned her around, pointing out from the shore. With the heels of the floats resting firmly on the sand, I tied her up for the night then cut some small branches from the fir trees to make a mattress. I built a fire and made tea, then went into the ration kit and got myself something to eat. It was getting dark. When camping out in the wilds, I would usually sit 'til about nine o'clock then "tuck in" until morning.

I was sitting there with my rifle beside me when a wolf howled. He was so close it seemed like he was no more than five feet behind my back. Then the whole pack started howling. The sound startled me so much I leapt right over the fire and was inside the aircraft in a flash. Now I was in a fine pickle, my rifle was still beside the fire. I looked around for quite a while but didn't see any wolves.

Luckily the wind was blowing the sparks from my fire out over the lake, so I didn't have to worry about the fire getting out of control.

Finally, after what seemed like hours, I climbed down from the plane and retrieved my rifle and sleeping bag. Dashing back, I spent the rest of the night in the aeroplane. The cockpit was not as comfortable as the bed I had made would have been, but at least I didn't have to worry about those critters gnawing on my bones.

Next morning the weather was much better. Before I left, I checked around the campfire, which, by that time, was out. I was surprised to see no sign of the wolves I had heard the night before. The snow that had fallen was dry so I didn't have too much trouble clearing off the wings as soon as it was light enough to take off.

Freeze-up came and the *Junkers* was switched from floats to ski landing gear. Later on that winter, I was sent north of Great Slave Lake. I flew up with the *Junkers* through Jasper, Edmonton, Fort McMurray, Fort Smith, and then on to Yellowknife. Fort Smith was the capital of the Northwest Territories until the seat of government was moved to Yellowknife in the mid 1960's.

I had been sent to assist the aircraft already stationed there in carrying freight into Port Radium. Each trip consisted of hauling four barrels of fuel into the mine on Great Bear Lake and hauling out uranium ore. The days were fairly short, so everyone was making one round-trip per day.

One winter, around 1947, I dropped in at Fort Ware to pick up the mail going in to Prince George. Art van Summers came in, in a hurry. He was going out to Prince George with his dog team and sled. All he had was his eiderdown and some dog food as well as some food for himself. On the lake, he'd been surrounded by a pack of wolves, which he thought, were probably after his dogs. We threw the sled and the dogs into the aircraft and I flew them to Prince George.

> Trappers, Natives and the government have found it necessary sometimes to control the wolf. There has been a lot of controversy about wolf kills in the North, about men trying to balance nature.

> Conservationists point out that wolves kill mainly the sick and elderly animals, "ensuring survival of the fittest". On the other hand, wolves would kill many of the caribou, which the Inuit and First Nations Peoples depended on for their food, clothing and shelter. Without the caribou the Natives would starve.

In the early 40's, I once saw seventeen herds of caribou between Yellowknife and Port Radium, on Great Slave Lake, heading north to go to the tundra. I was at five thousand feet and as far as I could see, they were coming, and as far as I could see, they were going. This went on for several days, so one can imagine the number of caribou back then. Later, in the 50's, I went up there and saw only one herd of caribou and it wasn't a very big one.

Some trappers had been over-hunting the caribou just to feed their dogs, rather than catching fish out of the lakes. With quite a few trappers stockpiling caribou, it's no wonder the herds had been almost wiped out. Spring was a bad time for the caribou because they'd go on some of the frozen lakes and the ice would break. Then they'd get stuck there. The trouble was that where one caribou went, all followed.

On the other hand, sometimes there can be just too many wolves. When wolves are faced with hunger, they have been known to attack sled dogs and sometimes people. I've never been able to think of the wolf as cute and cuddly, especially when in a pack. Perhaps Hollywood has contributed to the idea of wolves being gentle and loveable. A wolf bitch with cubs to feed will stop at nothing and wolves have terrorized many a lonely trapper in the night. Anyone who disagrees just needs to spend a night alone in subzero temperature with nothing for protection but a small campfire and perhaps a rifle. The howl of the wolf pack can be one of the most frightening sounds when one is alone in the North. Like with most things in life, some balance is always needed.

Although many people have been accustomed to not causing offence to Canadian First Nations, it might be useful to some readers for me to point out that "Inuit" is the name the Arctic people prefer for themselves. They have long detested the word "Eskimo", an Abenaki word meaning "eaters of raw meat". Those we called "Indians" cooked their meat and the two groups didn't associate with each other. Government schools, however, put all the aboriginal children together and forced them to speak English.

The people of the North have since been taking back their tribal names. The Anadai are Inuit from Anadai Lake. Further south are the Cree, Chippewan, Dogrib, Slavey, and many others. "First Nations Peoples" is a title far more acceptable today than the European misnomer "Indian".

Pat used the term Indian with full respect for the people he referred to, in a time less sensitive to the political correctness we know today.

STORIES AND RUMOURS

In the spring of '43, I was flying a *Junker GU 34* from Prince George into Fort Ware. I was doing the mail run up around Fort Ware about once a month. The *Hudson's Bay Company* store manager asked me to fly a load of provisions into Caribou Hide Lake, about 50 miles northwest of Fort Ware.

We were told that the Caribou Tribe Indians had killed a couple of white men and that an officer of the British Columbia Provincial Police had disappeared in that area. None of the pilots was willing to go.

I had flown into Two Brothers Lake, in that same area, with a load of supplies on an earlier occasion. I had just finished unloading and was about to leave, when a fellow came running down with one eye hanging out of its socket. He was desperate to get away from a group from the Caribou Hide Lake tribe. Apparently he had been involved with the Chief's daughter and was running for his life. I flew him into Prince George and made sure he got to the hospital to have his eye attended to. When the Hudson's Bay factor approached me about flying into Caribou Hide Lake, I hesitated as I thought it might be dangerous for me to go in there after having rescued that fellow from Native justice. However, the factor persisted and I finally agreed to go in.

An engineer by the name of Ed Handraddy used to fly with me. It was his job to tie up the plane as I brought her into shore. Well, this time he untied the plane then jumped ashore and I had to take off without him. I landed on Caribou Hide Lake alone. To my amazement the Chief called me by name and invited me up to his house. As I followed the Chief up the hill, I could see the curtains on each house being drawn aside. The people were all watching me. Well, I wasn't going to show them that I was scared and lose their respect. So I just went up there, walking tall. We had tea, then the

Chief gave me a list of groceries he wanted. He needed some sacks of flour and gave me some furs, telling me how much he wanted for them. The whole settlement had been starving, as there hadn't been any caribou for most of the winter.

When I got back, I told the Hudson's Bay factor he'd have to give what the Chief wanted for his furs or else I would not return. Well, I did go back.

My engineer still wouldn't come with me, but I took the supplies up to the Chief and he invited me up to the house again. His wife made fresh bread and we had tea and jam and cranberry pie and we got along just fine. I flew up there a couple of times after that. The Natives were always good to me.

In the summer of '47, I flew the Rocky Mountain Trench mail-run which went once a month. One of the stops on that route was Fort McLeod. The Indian Chief up there came into the general store where I was getting some supplies. He said: "I'm going to name you 'White Eagle', you're always flying and always helping people out."

I was sitting in the Prince George Hotel restaurant, when Sergeant Park of the Provincial Police came up to me and said: "Pat, I want you to go up to the trading post just east of Fort Nelson and pick up a gentleman by the name of Tommy Clarke, a fur-trader who has been accused of murdering one of the 'Indians'."

When I asked what police officer would be coming with me to make the arrest, I was told that I was to go up there alone and that the accused man would not give me any trouble.

That night, at the Fort Nelson trading post, I tried sleeping with one eye open, wondering if Tommy would kill me rather than go back to face charges. The next morning, Tommy got on the phone to one of his friends at the airport office. I heard him say that an "Indian" was coming in with some furs and that he would telephone back when he arrived. The fellow on the other end was to tell the Indian that it was God talking and that the Indian was to give all the furs to Tommy Clarke and to no one else.

When the Native trapper heard "God" speak to him on the telephone, his eyes went as big as saucers and he gave all his furs to Tommy.

Then Tommy told me that he didn't think he would be coming back with me, as he had too much to do. I told Tommy I would not go back without him, and that he would have to pay for every day I waited. He came back with me and was soon released for "lack of evidence". He was a real "gentleman", cheating those Native trappers and getting away with murder.

On another occasion, round about '52 or '53, I would fly a Chief out of Wood Buffalo Park in northern Alberta. As we flew above the clouds I remarked that we were in heaven. I told the Chief to have a good look around. "Maybe you'll even see God." I said, jokingly.

"I no see God", the Chief answered. I thought nothing of it until sometime later, when I heard a rumour from the Hudson's Bay factor, the Oblate Missionary was looking for me. On the Chief's pronouncement to his people that there was no god in heaven, all the Indians had stopped going to church. I feel bad about that now when I think of it. I never did get to meet the missionary priest, nor explain to the Chief that we don't see God in the simple way mission picture books might describe Him.

I was sent up to Fort St James to do some flying for Karl Hanawald. The trader had been a First-World-War officer with the German army. He had a trading post just north of Takla Lake, on a small lake called Bear Lake.

When I got up there, I pulled the plane in tail-first to shore and unloaded. Karl wasn't too happy. He'd lain awake on the floor all night while the Natives took potshots at his cabin. Sure enough there was a hole through the window and I could see where bullets had been shot into the door and walls. The Natives had made up an alcoholic brew and then, when sufficiently fired up, began taking potshots at Karl's cabin. Sometime later, I learned Karl had been selling ten cents worth of salt for sixty-five cents and that he was making huge profits on furs. The white man didn't always play fair in the North.

Early in the Second World War, a couple of German trappers were killed by a Native about forty miles north of Finlay Forks. Drunk on vanilla and alcohol and knowing Canada was at war with Germany, the Native reasoned the German trappers were also enemies. He did what he considered right and shot them.

Sometimes, when liquor was difficult to obtain, First Nations People drank vanilla extract. A common kitchen item, vanilla extract has a 35% alcohol content – a rather disgusting drink.

CANADIAN PACIFIC AIRLINES

Canadian Pacific Airlines bought out Canadian Airways in 1944, and I continued flying for the new company. That relationship was to continue until 1947. For a while, I was sent to Bowden, north of Calgary then back to the Coast, transporting mail, loggers, and others between Vancouver and Port Alice. I flew a couple of trips into the Queen Charlotte Islands and Campbell River just before Queen Charlotte Airlines became established.

> Queen Charlotte Airlines flew as a charter and scheduled service on the West Coast. The company evolved when Spillbery and Hepburn manufactured and serviced radios for logging camps and outports along the B.C. Coast. At first the company delivered and serviced radios by boat.

It was soon realized the use of aircraft would be much more efficient. Their service aircraft demonstrated a need for a regular commercial air-service in the area.

Very early in the spring of 1944, I was sent to Yellowknife. I went to Edmonton then north to Fort Smith. When I got to Fort Smith, the runway was covered in caribou. I tried chasing them off but they'd run in all directions and then scamper back again. Finally I managed to find a spot where I could get down, then taxied slowly up to the point where I could get some gas. By that time, the caribou were off into the bush.

When I got to Yellowknife, I found out they wanted me to fly fuel oil from Yellowknife into Port Radium. I was to take five barrels of fuel oil every trip. I started at daybreak and made two trips a day. The other pilots were only making one trip a day. Well, I wasn't very popular there for a while, but they'd sent me in to do a job and I was going to do the best I could. I worked there for about a month and the other pilots were able to make other trips that were more to their liking, so it worked out fine.

The uranium mine was on the East side of Great Bear Lake. My manager came down with some men who carried what I thought were sacks of rock. The manager gave me the name of a man I was to call in Yellowknife and he instructed that I was to say nothing about what I was carrying. Later on, I was to find out that what I had carried was some of the uranium ore that was eventually used to make the bomb that was dropped on Japan. By that time, it was too late for me to worry about my small part in that tragedy.

I was sent to Anahim Lake, southwest of Prince George, to pick up "Panhandle" Phillips who ran a big cattle ranch in that area. He had been kicked by a stallion he was always riding and had broken his hip.

I had to stay overnight, because it would have been too dark to land in Vanderhoof. PanHandle's wife recognized me as having once carried groceries home for her way back when I was instructing in Richmond. "It's a small world!"

THE YOUNG ENGINEER

In the spring of 1946, I was on floats and was sent in to McConnell Lakes, about one- hundred-and-fifty miles north-by-north-east of Fort St James, to bring in some supplies to a prospector. Russ Baker asked me to take a mining engineer who had just completed university along on the trip so he could experience flying in the bush. We unloaded the prospector's supplies, then took off and climbed to nine thousand feet. We had gone some distance when the engine cut out. There was not a lake in sight.

I knew that Lake Johanesson was nestled behind the mountain range and I knew of a spot between the mountains where I could get through to the lake. I rounded the corner of the mountain just clearing the ridge. The lake was frozen over and I was on floats. I turned to the young engineer and said, "Boy, this looks like our last ride". I had never before had to land a floatplane on ice.

I touched down with what seemed to be the smoothest landing I'd ever made in my life. However, on the ice I had no control and the aircraft made a left turn towards the bank, which stopped the plane.

There was about two inches of water over the ice and we had a trailing- antenna we could run out when we wanted to call. We rolled the antenna out and the engineer went to the end and held it up. I pressed the mike button to tell Fort St. James I was down on the lake. The young engineer received a pretty strong shock, because he was standing in water. He took the pillow from my seat and draped the wire over it but still got a shock. Across the lake, I knew a miner by the name of Carl Springer had a cache containing food and a tent. So we rolled up the trailing-antenna and walked about a mile across the lake. We put up a tent and spent the next day waiting for searchers to begin looking. No one showed up.

On the second morning we boiled some rice and trekked up over the glacier to Aiken Lake, fifty miles north by north west of Fort St. James. There was a trapper there with lots of supplies and a radio. We could then contact Fort St. James. We climbed the mountain with snow up to our knees. Halfway down the other side, we heard Russ Baker taking off with the *Junkers*. We got to the cabin just before dark. Next day Russ flew in and picked us up. About a week later he flew me back in with a mechanic and we fixed the engine and got the plane out of there.

LIGHTING THE WAY

One day in 1945, I had a call to go in to Finlay Forks to pick up Marjorie MacDougal, who was very ill.

It was getting quite late in the day, so I said to Roy MacDougal "I think we'd better wait 'til morning because it's getting pretty late right now."

He said "No. I want you to take her in right now, because she's very sick and I'm worried about her."

Marjorie was crying with pain. So I gave in and said, "Well, Okay I'll make a go for it."

We didn't get half way to Fort Smith, before it was pitch black. This was my first time ever doing any night flying. Luckily, I had taken some link training.

Link training is a form of instrument training, starting as far back as the 1930's, in a darkened mock-up of a cockpit.

I continued up the Parsnip River, then got onto the Crooked River and cut up to Summit Lake. That was all open and I knew the course from Summit Lake into Prince George, so I kept going. Then I saw the beacon light up at the Prince George airport.

I got over Prince George and there was a railroad bridge that passed over the Fraser River. I passed over the bridge and turned to come in low, with my landing lights close to the shoreline, so that I'd know how far away the water was. Then four cars put their lights on. Well, that was fine because I could see the bank, and everything, clearly. I was just about ready to land when all the lights went out. There I was back in the dark again, so I circled down slowly until I saw the bank again and followed along to the dock. Walter Gilbert, one of the senior partners of the company, had told those car drivers to put their lights out because he thought the light would blind me as I came in. Well, he didn't know it had just the opposite effect, because their lights were shining across the river onto the far bank. Finally, I got in safely and picked Marjorie up in my arms and took her to the hospital.

I ALMOST JOIN THE AIR FORCE

I was sent out to pick up two stretcher cases at Selkirk. On my way back with the patients, I ran into a severe snowstorm over Lac Laberge. (*Not to be confused with Lac Laberge in Northern Quebec.*) I knew that a night in the cold would be disastrous for my two patients, so it became imperative that I make Whitehorse. Whitehorse was in a whiteout condition, so I called the tower requesting landing lights be put on as I could see straight down.

> *A whiteout is a weather condition caused by a heavy cloud-cover over the snow. The light coming from above is just about equal to the light reflected from below, which causes an absence of shadow and makes the horizon invisible.*

The fellow in the tower became very excited and talked so fast I could not understand him. It was evident later, he had been trying to get an Air Force machine to hold; at the same time he was asking me to hold over town. The Air Force machine took off just as I came in for a landing and I bounced out of his way into deep snow at the side of the runway. However, I got out of this and the patients were taken to warm beds in the hospital. That was about the closest I ever came to joining the Air Force.

In the spring of '43, I ferried a *Fairchild '82* from Fort St James to Winnipeg and, as occasionally happened, my wife accompanied me for what was to be her furthest trip east. Somewhere just west of Winnipeg, we lost our oil pressure and had to put down at a wartime Air Force base.

As I approached the runway, red flares and blue lights flashed in every direction. Thinking that, in my emergency situation, I had the right-of-way, I touched down just as an R.C.A.F. trainer tried to land on my tail. I swung to the grass and stopped. I then walked back to the tower where I was severely reprimanded. However, they did accept my explanation.

We left the aircraft there and took a bus to Winnipeg. Winnipeg was windy and very boring. After a couple of days, we picked up another *Fairchild*. This time the compass gave out over Saskatchewan. Jean became very airsick as she watched the compass needle spin round and round. We kept going by following railroad and other markers I knew, until we got to Charley Lake, just out of Fort St. John. The next day, with the compass still going wild, we flew on to Fort St. James and, to Jean's relief, home.

CENTRAL B.C. AIRWAYS

In 1947, Russ Baker and Walter Gilbert asked me if I would fly for them in their new company Central B.C. Airways. I thought about it for a while. I had my ticket for night flying and a public transport ticket but I didn't seem to be able to get onto the big aircraft. They always sent me to fly in the bush. So I thought, "Oh well, if I'm going to fly in the bush, I may as well do it for Russ Baker and Walter Gilbert.

> Central B.C. Airways acquired several other operations and later formed Pacific Western (P.W.A.). The process was repeated with the notable acquisition being Pacific Airlines (C.P.A.). The new company became Canadian Airlines International (C.A.I.).

Russ and Walter sent me to Winnipeg to pick up a *Fox Moth*. That was on a Friday and the plane was not yet on floats. They were just hoisting it. *A Fox Moth is not a very big machine. The pilot sat out in the open, halfway*

113

back in the aeroplane. I had no helmet and no goggles with me. I remember thinking this was a rather small aircraft to start an airline with. "Start small - end up big"

The next morning I checked her over thoroughly, and took her for a test run. Then I headed up to The Pas. Seeing that this plane was on floats, I thought I should take the northern route where there were more lakes, rather than fly over the bald prairie. I arrived in The Pas, landing there at about lunchtime on Sunday. The base was empty. There was not a plane, nor a person in sight. I went to a restaurant in town to get a bite to eat and to try to find the base manager. Finally, I got the base manager's name and phoned him. He arrived after two o'clock and I was able to get some fuel. At last, I took off and flew a bit north-of-due-west for Cooking Lake, southeast of Edmonton. At Cooking Lake, the base manager was out and I had to wait for him. After quite a while, I decided to check in at the motel and fly out the next morning.

When I met Walter Gilbert in Prince George, he told me another pilot was going to take that plane to do the Rocky Mountain Trench mail run and I was to go to another job out of Fort Saint James. I went by bus to Vanderhoof, then travelled the rest of the way by *stagecoach. (This was a large car, not a relic of the Old West.)*

THE AIR FORCE NORSEMAN

After settling into the small hotel and having something to eat, I thought I'd take a stroll down to the base. Once again, there was nobody around and no aircraft. A couple of days later, a *Royal Canadian Air Force Norseman* flew in. This plane bore R.C.A.F. insignia and carried no commercial identification. I spoke to Lorne Usher and he told me this was the plane I'd be flying for a while. The plane had been heavily used and there were neither engine logbooks nor aircraft logbooks. Lorne handed me a journey logbook and told me that, next morning, I was to take off for Stewart, B.C., with one passenger. I tried to get acquainted with the fellow at the hotel, but he just wasn't friendly, so I left him alone. The next day, he was on the plane and we flew to Stewart. There I met the manager of the mining exploration for whom I would be flying.

The man I had flown in was a Mr. Coulter, the superintendent of a big mining company that was doing the exploration for the MacKay mine. Mr. Coulter was also Mr. MacKay's financial backer. I met Tommy MacKay, owner and superintendent of the company, and the next morning he had a load sent down to the aircraft for me and I started flying.

I flew quite a few loads of supplies into MacKay Lake until they didn't need any more supplies. Mr.

Coulter said he would like to come along and take his wife on the last trip in. The plane was a bit too heavy, so I decided to leave as much as I could behind. I gave the engineer my supply kit and my briefcase, (forgetting to remove my wallet), I even gave him my eiderdown and then I figured we were just right for takeoff.

I dropped off the supplies at the lake, and then took off with Mr. and Mrs. Coulter for Stewart. We had just passed the glacier, when I found out the rest of the passes were all closed in. So I had to follow the Leduc River down until it went into the ocean and then, into Ketchikan Alaska.

I stopped at the dock and reported in. I also knew I'd have to get some gas to get back to Stewart. Well, the dock crew wouldn't gas me up. Instead they phoned and got the Customs people down. A Customs officer put me in one room, and Mr. and Mrs. Coulter in another. Then they came back to me and asked me if I knew anybody in Alaska. I said: "No, sir. I've never been in Alaska before in my life."

There I was with a Canadian Air Force Plane, no logbook and no identification papers. A plane that could not be accounted for could mean big trouble.

Fortunately, on that trip, I happened to have two very important passengers with me. One was Mr. Coulter, the superintendent of the MacKay Exploration outfit. The other was his wife who wanted a little excitement before returning home to England. Mr. Coulter's identity was confirmed by the bank manager in Ketchikan, and I was off the hook. As I didn't have any money for necessary expenses, including refuelling, the bank manager lent me fifty dollars, which I repaid later through my own account in Hyder, Alaska, just across the border from Stewart. I sure was lucky; those Americans treated me very well. Next morning the weather was still low, so I had to fly down the coast to the Portland Canal then follow that up to Stewart. From Stewart, I headed back for Fort St. James.

The Air Force finally took back their *Norseman*. Russ Baker bought several planes from *Canadian Pacific Airlines*, mostly *Junkers JU34*. This made me feel a lot more confident, because I knew these planes had been well cared for.

It was at this time that the company name was changed to *Pacific Western*. I guess, I was the first pilot for *Pacific Western*, although at first we were known as *Central B.C. Airways*. I did the Rocky Mountain Trench Run, delivering freight, mail and passengers from Prince George to Fort Ware, with stops at Fort MacLeod, Finlay Forks, and Fort Graham.

THE CAMP COOK

Following my adventures in Alaska, I went in to do some flying for Tom MacKay, taking in groceries to the MacKay mine. Mr. Harris, Superintendent of the Summit Lake Gold Mines, came to me and asked me to fly some supplies into his camp.

> Summit Lake is on the east side of the Salmon Glacier. Big chunks of ice would frequently fall from the glacier into the lake.

The only time I could get in there was when there was a west wind blowing, which would blow all the icebergs against the east shore. It was a very deep lake and some of those icebergs were as big as apartment buildings.

After about four trips, Mr. Harris came to me and told me the cook was in town and roaring drunk. He asked me to pick up the cook and fly him back to the camp. Well, the tide in Stewart was way out and we couldn't use the ramp to reach the plane so we had to use the ladder. I used a rope, which I tied like a cage around the cook, and then I hooked the rope around a winch, and slowly lowered him down from the high bank onto a float. He was a big man and by this time he was out cold. It took five of us to put him into the aeroplane.

I landed on Summit Lake and unloaded all the groceries. In the meantime the cook came-to and asked: "Where am I?" I said, "You're in camp". Well he didn't want to be in camp, he wanted to be back in town. I told him Mr. Harris had told me not to bring him back. He was grumbling so I suggested we go up and get a cup of coffee, and talk the matter over. There was a 4" X 12" plank to the shoreline from the float. I offered to help him ashore, but he was quite cantankerous and said he could make it on his own. Anyway, he got about halfway across the plank and fell into the cold water. I grabbed him by the collar of his shirt and dragged him ashore. His language was getting quite abusive but he had to go up to the cabin to change his clothes. Halfway up the hill, I told him I had to go back to get something from the plane. I went back down and pushed her out and flew back to Stewart.

The next day when I got back to camp the cook sent word he wanted me to go and have a cup of coffee with him. I thought it would be better to stay clear of him for a while, so I declined.

THE FLYING HORSE

In my day I have flown hives of bees, chickens, beavers, and a planeload of savage sled- dogs. Once, they needed a packhorse flown from Stewart to a camp on MacKay Lake. MacKay Lake is a small lake, a bit below four thousand feet. At that time, this was someone else's territory, but everyone said the job couldn't be done.

I told them, "If you want the horse in, I'll try it. If it can't be done, it won't be done."

That was my answer and as good as a "yes" to them.

Bill Crawford had a pack train of horses, so I asked him to get the smallest and quietest and maybe the oldest horse he could find so there wouldn't be too much trouble in the air. Well, Bill brought down a horse I was sure was over the maximum weight I could take. Not only that, they had no tranquilizer for the beast. This was going to be quite a ride. I asked Bill Crawford, the horse's owner, to "throw the horse" so we could tie his legs before hoisting him onto the plane. Well, neither Bill nor anyone else there knew how to throw a horse (*meaning to throw it onto its side*).

I took some rope and gently secured the animal. The trick was to get the horse down, tie her legs and get her into a cargo net.

It took ten men to lift the animal into the plane headfirst. At first, we had too much weight at the back of the plane; the floats were under the water, so we had to turn the horse around. Then we stripped out all the other gear. The door wouldn't close, so we'd have to fly with the door off. I told the cowboy to put on a warm jacket but he was hot from helping to load the horse and wouldn't listen to me. There was no time to argue. With him sitting on the horse's head to keep her down and braced, and to keep her from sliding back, we took-off.

We had to circle three times around Stewart before we could get enough height to clear the mountain. We landed at MacKay Lake with one frozen cowboy. There was nobody to help us unload so the three of us slid the horse off and I untied her, gave her a slap on the rump, and she went up the hill and began eating grass as if nothing had ever happened.

The only sad part to this story is the fact that we couldn't get that horse back out when winter came because the lake was too small for takeoff with so much added weight. Because she would not have survived the winter snow and cold, she had to be shot.

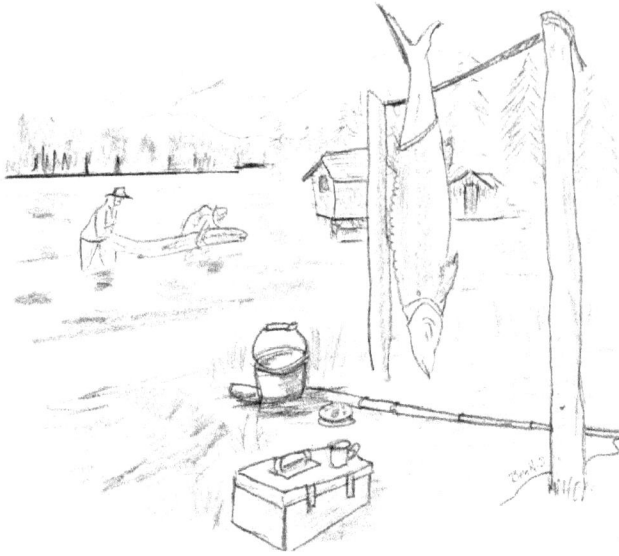

THE HAPPY LIFE

The early 1940's were happy days, spent skimming along at ninety miles an hour, sometimes just above the tree tops, following logging-roads hacked out of the wilderness in northern B.C. In those days there were very few roads, and the railroads had not yet come that far north. Passengers would hold on to their hats as I banked my little pontooned *Beaver*, to come in against the wind and tie up at a dock by a bush-camp at the edge of the Peace River. Passengers would then have to walk across a heaving narrow plank to the wharf. There I would unload the cargo: several cases of beer, bottles of rye and gin, mail and city grocery orders.

Sometimes, in the summer months, I would hedgehop passengers and cargo seven days a week out of Fort Smith on the Slave River – just across the Alberta border in the North West Territories. Sometimes bush pilots would see a white sheet laid out on the ground or draped over the roof of a lonely outpost. This was the universal distress signal in the North. We would always go out of our way to check for those in distress. We would fly over and come in on a tiny lake or on a stretch of river, sometimes to bring out a sick child or an injured trapper.

At times, if the schedule permitted, I would set down on a lake and catch a trout or two to bring home to my wife, Jean, who was always waiting for me in Fort Smith. Jean and I had been married a week before Christmas in 1945, in Vancouver. I'd take a quick buzz over the house before landing so she'd know I was on my way home.

Once in a while, I was able to surprise Jean with a beautiful gift. One such gift was a magnificent sweater hand knitted by the Coast Salish women from the Cowichan Valley on Vancouver Island. The Salish wove clothing and blankets using the hair of a small wool dog, sometimes mixed with mountain goat wool and goose down. The wool dog was a special breed, owned by the women of the village and kept separate from the hunting dogs. The women sheared the dogs with a mussel shell knife. The hair was so thick, they said they could lift it by one corner like a rug. The dogs were sheared two or three times each summer. Mountain goat wool was good because it was fine, straight and very soft.

Jean still wears her Cowichan sweater on cool nights. It's probably the best gift I ever gave her.

Today, Cowichan sweaters are made from black sheep wool.

Much of my time was my own and, in many ways, I was my own boss. When I wanted fish, I could land on a lake and catch my supper. I was never one to be padlocked to a desk, nor to any nine-to-five job in the big city. I did not feel the need to conform.

At other times, I might have to work around the clock ferrying firefighters into a bad bush-fire, skimming over treetops through billowing smoke to find a landing site. Landing in the dark on an unlit river was always risky. Then getting close enough to shore for passengers to disembark would be even trickier. I would run as far into the reeds as I could go, then the fire-fighters would have to make their way ashore, through mud and water, with packs held high. Meanwhile, I'd turn and take off in a steep incline, to fetch another group.

Park rangers in the Northwest Territories and in northern Alberta and B.C. used to call me "Wet Handkerchief Carey" because they said I could almost land on a wet handkerchief, while ferrying supplies and firefighters into the bush.

In early winter, it was sometimes difficult to tell if the ice on a lake was thick enough to land on. The bush pilot would bump down and take off again, then look to see if the impact of his skis had left open water. If there was open water, then we'd have to look for another lake.

Sometimes I would have to remove two of the four seats in the little *Beaver* to be able to carry a cargo of nails and other hardware. Passengers would find themselves propped up against duffel bags and packing cases.

Once, I had to fly two drunken Swedes to Port Alice. Because of the weather, I was flying just above the treetops. Suddenly the aeroplane was shaking. I looked back to see one of the fellows relieving himself at the open door. I yelled. "Shut the #*@$% door!"

I must say a word for my good wife, Jean. Bush pilot wives are a hardy bunch. Very often, they must live in near wilderness to be close to their husbands. Women who prefer the big city should marry lawyers or bankers.

In stormy weather, the bush pilot wife might worry that her husband will make it down safely.

Sad and frightening gatherings are at funerals and memorial services for pilot friends killed in the bush or in high mountains. Apart from empathizing with the new widow, "This could have been my Ayliffe," will surely cross her mind.

Bush pilot wives live and breathe aviation and probably know more about aircraft than many people who work in airports and airline offices today. Jean lived my dream every day of our married life and she got to know many of the other pilot's wives even if she didn't get to see them all that often.

Whenever things aren't going all that well at home, the pilot's wife remembers she, like her husband, takes off against the wind, not with it.

The pilot is lucky to have such a good wife. She's home when the kids are sick while he's free as a bird above the clouds. No crying kids, dirty diapers nor snotty noses for him. Bush pilot wives learn to live independent lives when their husbands are away. They raise the children mostly alone and sometimes go through life's events such as births and deaths alone.

While I was flying here and there, Jean tended our vegetable garden, then prepared and canned vegetables and fruit just as her mother and my mother had done. I usually had a good supply of logs put by for winter fires and for the kitchen stove whenever we lived without electricity. Jean still had to chop kindling and many times wash clothes by hand. I'd fly over and see the sheets hanging on the clothesline, flapping in the breeze.

Although pilots who fly for major airlines today make pretty good salaries, bush pilots in the 40s, 50s and 60s had to keep their belts fairly tight, especially those of us with families to feed. Jean had to do her fair share of scrimping and saving to make ends meet. I can't remember either of us ever complaining. However, on hind thought, life must have been fairly tough for our stay at home wives in those days. Jean belonged to a breed of tough women. Whenever life became overwhelming, she always knew to point her nose into the wind and fly.

TRIAL IN THE NORTH

"Requiem for Margaret Poole"

A lot of people have forgotten that we had our own Provincial Police in British Columbia from 1858 until 1950. Back in 1943, there was a murder at Fort Ware, a lonely snowbound outpost, two hundred miles north of Prince George. A Native snowshoed eighty miles to Finlay Forks to get the message radioed out through the Hudson's Bay trader. I was asked to pick up Sergeant Clark, Game Warden Jank and special constable "Skook" Davidson from Prince George and fly them up to Fort Ware to investigate and bring out the killer.

> *"Skook" is short for Skookum, which is a Chinook word meaning strong. Skook Davidson was strong.*

> *Mount Skook Davidson, 2,382 metres (7,815 ft), in the Kechika Range of the Cassiar Mountains in far northern B.C. is named after the same famous First World War hero, Special Constable, horse packer, rancher and land surveyor, John Skook Davidson, pioneer of the north.*

Bad weather forced us to land at Finlay Forks, where we dug out a drum of gasoline from the drifts at the edge of the Finlay River and hand-pumped the fuel into the plane. Meanwhile the ceiling dropped further, until we had no choice but to remain for three days while a blizzard raged about us. When the storm died down sufficiently, we hand-cleared a strip and took off again. The ceiling was still so low we had to hedgehop our way up the frozen river to Fort Ware. Fort Ware consisted of a Hudson's Bay store, a fur cache and warehouse, a cabin for stopover trappers and a cabin for store manager Jack Copeland, his wife and two children.

The murder investigation got immediately underway. A member of the Beaver Tribe had clubbed his wife to death with a rifle-butt, then told everyone around the post she had frozen to death. Some people didn't believe the story. The body had been buried and the suspected killer was back out on the trap-line. We left constable Davidson to round up witnesses and to await the return of the suspect. It was decided the others should fly out rather than risk getting snowed in for an indeterminate length of time. With Clark and Jank, I soon took to the air but had to refuel once more at Finlay Forks. As the snow got heavy, we knew we would have to stay put in a nearby vacant cabin.

By the next morning, a " Peace River Wind" was funnelling down the canyon. We anchored the plane with cables attached to full drums of gasoline and managed to lash a canvas covering over the engine and wings. For five more days the wind howled.

It finally cleared enough for us to go out to the plane. We found her covered in ice and snow. After much work, we were able to set blow-pots on the ice and began to warm the engine-oil, which I had drained from the plane when we first landed. When the oil was steaming, we poured it back, but still the plane would not start. I worked on that plane all through the next night but to no avail. Then I discovered the cylinder head was cracked. Fortunately we had a radio on board and I promptly reported our plight.

Ten days later, after countless games of cribbage and long being out of flapjacks and bacon, we got word a new cylinder head would be delivered the following day. By that time, the wind had blown our plane, anchors and all, a hundred yards along the ice, and the snow, banked against her, had taken on the consistency of cement. I was left with the new cylinder head, while Clark and Jank were whisked off to Prince George to arrange for the inquest.

On March 2nd, 1943, "Skook" Davidson sent word from Fort Ware, to police headquarters in Prince George, that he had Poole, the man accused of killing his wife, under his wing. I was to take Bill Harris, who would act as magistrate, and Captain J.C. Dawson, who was to be the doctor, from the nearby army camp. I was also to bring along Sgt. Clarke, and "Indian Agent" Bob Howe, as well as a mechanic.

We flew back to Fort Ware. The body of Margaret Poole was exhumed and Dr. Dawson performed a hasty post-mortem on the frozen corpse. In one of the cabins, Magistrate Harris conducted a preliminary hearing. That night, in the same building, a jury was sworn in and, considering the weather, told to "make it snappy". With the jury's pronouncement of "guilty", Poole was formally charged with the murder. As the group filed out at about 11:30 that night, the Native quietly remarked that his wife had been left exposed up on the hill. "What if she get eaten by wolves?" he said.

The group hastily reassembled up at the top of the hill and closing up the coffin, reburied Margaret Poole.

At around midnight, in the middle of that simple graveyard, "Skook" Davidson suggested a soldier's farewell. With that he drew his gun and solemnly fired six shots into the air. Then from the pocket of his pea jacket, George Clark produced a mickey of rum, which was passed around until empty. A timber wolf howled and Clarke commented: "Requiem for Margaret Poole".

It is a sad comment on our contribution to the civilizing of our Native Peoples that if one of the white traders had not been carrying on with the wife of a Native in the first place, this unfortunate incident would not have occurred. Poole was later hanged.

ASSOCIATED AIRWAYS - 1952

For a while, I took a break from flying, to work for Bert Tremblay on the Columbia Cellulose booming grounds near Terrace, B.C. After the camp closed down, I thought I'd take the opportunity to go to Edmonton to take my Diesel Diploma practical exam for which I had been preparing for quite some time. I was all ready but the day before we were to write our exams, King George VI died, so it was decided to close the school down for the day.

I was sitting around in the boarding house where I was staying and feeling bored, so I decided to go out to the airport to see what was going on. While I was wandering around the airport, I saw an *Associated Airways* sign and thought to myself: "I wonder if they need any pilots."

I went into the office and there was Tommy Fox, whom I had already known in Vancouver. Tommy wanted me to fly right away, but I told him I was to write my diesel exam the next day.

After the exam, I had to go back to Prince Rupert to get all the household furniture out of the float-house and get it packed. The school told me I could have a job as a railway- engineer with one of the railways out of Toronto. However, I had already accepted to go back to flying, and that was what I wanted to do. I shipped the family furniture from Prince Rupert to Edmonton, then caught one of the *Associated Airways* flights up to Yellowknife.

I flew out of Yellowknife for a while. Then *Associated Airways* sent me to Fort Smith, on the Slave River, where I remained for several years.

NATIVE PEOPLES OF THE NORTH

Pilots didn't like flying for the government. I used to do things my way but always let them think it was their idea – then everyone was happy.

The Inuit from Ennadai Lake were hunting caribou close to Baker Lake, out towards Hudson Bay, but the herd did not come through that year and the people were starving. I was sent in to deliver buffalo meat from the government roundup at Wood Buffalo Park. The Inuit preferred caribou, as that was the taste they had always been used to, however they ate the buffalo meat when there was nothing else. When I flew up there they were living in tents made of caribou skins, which were rotting in the rain. Everything got wet. Sometimes the children would be running around naked getting bitten by mosquitoes. I began scrounging for clothes for them.

Ennadai Lake, Nunavut, is 52 mi (84 km) long by 3 to 14 mi (4.8 to 23 km) wide.

I remember a little girl who had been born with a clubfoot. The Inuit thought that this was an evil thing, so they cut the child's foot off. The *Royal Canadian Mounted Police* took her to hospital. Another time, on a hunting trip, a girl shot herself in the foot. The people just left her there sitting on a rock. When the tribe got back to Ennadai Lake, they reported to the Sergeant of the Signal Corps who called the *R.C.M.P.* in Fort Smith. The *R.C.M.P.* then flew out and picked up the young girl, bringing her to hospital in Fort Smith.

I flew First Nations and Inuit children to residential schools in Fort Smith, Fort Resolution, and in Yellowknife, on Great Slave Lake.

The government thought residential schools would be more cost-efficient than trying to run numerous little schools. However, we now know that, in the attempt to give the Native Peoples a white man's education, we stripped our First Canadians of their own heritage. The children could no longer be influenced by their parents in their own small villages. Instead they took on the white man's values. Native children would be sent home for two months in the summer. However, the summer was not the time for learning the difficult part of survival techniques. A lot of the knowledge of the original ways was probably lost in one generation.

The white man was up in those areas mainly for the mineral resources. The younger members of the communities had to leave when the white man left, because they no longer knew the old ways. We now know that, unfortunately, some people in those schools also took advantage of the Native children when they were without much protection. This was more a case of certain individuals at fault, not the schools in general.

Almost all the teachers I got to know in those days were kind and genuinely interested in their charges. They had to be good people to volunteer to teach in isolated conditions for such low wages.

At the beginning of the school year I would fly new teachers in. Once that cold weather hit, a few of them had second thoughts about teaching in the North and some didn't last more than a few months. We were used to the cold. Of course we were all dressed up in sealskin outfits. In 1954, I had brought some skins back from the Arctic coast and had them tanned in Edmonton. Then I cut out patterns and made clothing for myself and for each of our children. I bought about a hundred muskrat skins and had a fur coat made for Jean. I used the remainder to make a parka for our daughter, Colleen.

We had three children. One of our sons had been hit by a car and killed when we lived in Fort Smith.

When there were caribou below the timberline, the government decided to move the Inuit to the woods so they could hunt for meat. The trees would snap in the cold and the Natives thought that it was the devil in the trees making the noise. The headman told the Signal Corps interpreter "Not only did the trees go 'boom!' but they kept moving in front of the caribou, so we could not hunt them."

Sometimes I would fly the Inuit hunters to the caribou and I would chase the caribou towards them with my plane. Then they would all begin shooting, and some would shoot high and I had to nose up fast, so as not to be shot down by stray bullets.

After the Canadian Army Signal Corps built the radio station at Ennadai Lake in 1949, and in a paternalistic effort to solve the occasional Innuit starvation problem, the Canadian government began relocating the Ahiarmiut from Ennadai Lake to various communities distanced from one to the other. Administration decisions regarding relocation were based on economic factors. The government did not want the Innuit, who had begun to enjoy trade in guns, tobacco and other goods, to become dependent on relief in times of scarcity and lose their ability to survive independently.

The first relocation was to Nueltin Lake in 1950 another to Henik Lake in 1957. Other Ahiarmiut were relocated to Arviat and from Arviat to Whale Cove and Rankin Inlet. Testimonies of the Ahiarmiut elders recorded in Arviat show these relocations were experienced as a painful and terrible deportation.

HERDING BUFFALO FROM THE AIR

Wood Buffalo Park is just below Great Slave Lake, on the border between northern Alberta and the Northwest Territories. It is the largest buffalo preserve on the continent. The park extends from Fort Smith, near the northeast corner of the Alberta border, across to Buffalo Lake, down to Ft. Chippewan on Lake Athabaska, and to the Fifth Meridian on the Peace River.

Every year the herd would have to be culled, so park rangers would organize a buffalo kill. In 1954, buffalo meat was selling for seventy cents a pound for choice cuts, however, most of the meat was reserved for the Indians and Inuit of the North.

It was my job to get behind the herd with my red and yellow ski plane and dive at the buffalo to send them stampeding into the corral. This was considered one of the toughest flying missions of the North. First thing in the morning we'd be out chipping the ice from the plane. Sometimes this would take a couple of hours. We'd fly four-hour shifts, twice a day, looking for buffalo, then dive down at them like sheepdogs biting at their heels. Very often, we'd be just twenty to thirty feet off the ground. Sometimes we'd come in with bits of twigs caught in the fuselage. One wrong turn and a whole herd of frantic beasts would be off into the bush. It could be very frustrating at times because groups of buffalo would gallop off in various directions and often there seemed to be no way to keep the herd together.

At the corral, Cree sharpshooters would pick out certain animals, then skinners and butchers would set to work completing the job in very quick time.

Our annual roundup culled about five hundred of the more than twenty thousand buffalo in the park.

> This process was more humane than the buffalo hunts of the 1800's, when whole herds were slaughtered, just for buffalo tongue and trophies. In modern times, no part of the animal is wasted. Even the horns are used for Native carvings.

THE PET MOOSE

The game warden at Hay Camp, Gordie Carlson, was being transferred to Pine Lake. He had rescued a young moose, which had been found trapped amongst some fallen trees in a creek. Gordie had taken the wounded and frightened animal home and nursed it back to health. Now the moose followed him everywhere. It was like a pet and he wanted to bring it with him, as he was afraid it was not yet ready to survive on its own in the wild.

I was worried his sharp hoofs would damage the floats, so the two of us had to lift the moose onto the plane. I never thought I'd be flying a wild moose.

After dropping Gordie and his pet off at their new location, I walked along the float to get back up on the aeroplane and the moose followed me, wanting to get back on the plane with me. I had to lead him back to shore and Gordie held him behind a building while I took off.

GLACIER GRIZZLY

When I was flying out of Stewart, around 1964, Jack Campbell, a foreman for the Grand Duc Mining Company, asked me to fly up on the glacier and pick up a couple of batteries and a radio out of the cabins they had used when they were drilling to find the depth of the glacier.

> Surveyors ascertained the deepest part of the ice was 2,227 feet. The engineers had to know that because they were cutting an eleven-mile tunnel underneath that glacier from Tide Lake, down to the Leduc camp and had to have sufficient rock above to provide necessary support. The engineers ran into a seam of soapstone and the tunnel kept collapsing, until steel girders and cement support works were put in place.
>
> Tide Lake, just east of Summit Lake and north of Stewart, was formed in prehistoric times by a "moraine", an accumulation of boulders, stones, and other debris carried and deposited by a glacier. In more recent flooding, some years before the Grand Duc Mining Company's arrival, the dam had washed out and left the lake-bed dry.

It was in August, when I went up to pick up the batteries and radio. During the summer the sun had melted all the ice on the south side of the building and it had fallen over. So the front door was where the roof should have been.

I got out of the aircraft very carefully because in August some of the bridges over the crevasses would be very thin and a person could easily fall through. As I got near the cabin, a glacier grizzly came out from under the building, sauntered round the corner and looked at me.

I looked at him and I was gone. I tell you it didn't take me long. I wasn't worrying about any crevasses or anything; I was getting back into that aeroplane.

The bear stood up and looked at me so I started up the engine thinking the noise would scare him off. Well, he just stood there. So I just had to wait until that bear finally ambled off. I shudder to think of what that huge creature could have done to the aircraft had he been sufficiently aroused. I would have been stranded on the ice, if I were still alive by that time.

When I was sure the bear was well away, I took some rope out of the plane so I could get into the cookhouse with the door on the topside.

I secured one end of the rope then climbed down inside the "upset cabin" and tied the batteries to the rope end, one at a time, and climbed back up, then hauled all the equipment up to what was now the roof. I made sure each time I went up there to have a good look around to make sure that bear wasn't around.

Finally I lowered the batteries and the radio down from the "roof" to the glacier, then loaded them into the plane and took off to Stewart. I was sure glad to get out of there.

CAT – PIECE BY PIECE

About 1962, a mining engineer named Eric Ostensoe was managing a mine in Snippiker Creek, north of Stewart. He needed a small caterpillar tractor – I believe a D-7 – that was at Shaft Creek, south of the village of Telegraph Creek, and wanted me to bring it in to him piece by piece.

The first to go up was the engine. Then I took the tracks up, one at a time. The tracks, when rolled up tight, were about four-and-a-half feet high and very heavy. We had planks on the bottom of the aircraft so there would be no danger of something going through the floor. We winched the engine up with a "come-along", a portable chain-hoist. It took five men to load the plane. Then we had to tie everything down very securely.

It took six trips to get that cat in there. The plane I was flying was an *Otter* and the mining company had only a short strip at Snippiker Creek – four hundred feet. With such a heavy load I was lucky to get it in there and told Eric he'd have to lengthen the runway for me to get that machinery back out again. He used the cat to lengthen the strip, and we eventually flew the cat back to Shaft Creek.

Boy, that was hard work.

BRINGING IN A BOAT

A prospecting outfit came to me in 1968. They had tried to fly a boat in to a creek a bit north of Leduc near Stewart, with a helicopter. The boat was about four feet by twelve feet. It got so rough when the wind caught the boat that the helicopter pilot had to let it go. The boat smashed up on the rocks below. So they came to me and asked if I could take one in. I said, "We'll tie it underneath the aeroplane and give it a try." They brought the boat in and Bill Ross, my son Robert and I tied that boat under the plane. We only had about four inches of clearance between the bottom of the boat and the ground. The runway we had to come in on was a gravel creek-bed.

I flew up the creek a couple of miles then turned and came in as low as I could and progressively slowed the aircraft. First of all I put down the partial flap and adjusted the power.

Finally, about half-a-mile back, the stall warning-light, which had been blinking on and off, came on steady. I had to keep boosting the power to keep her flying, while bringing her lower and lower. We landed on the main gear and rolled practically the whole length of the runway before the rear-wheel came down. At the end of the runway, there was a huge pile of logs. We stopped within a couple of feet of those logs and just had room to turn around and run back to where the men were waiting to unload the boat.

My son looked later at the brake skid-marks. We had touched down within ten feet of the beginning of that runway. A couple of feet more at the other end and we would have lost our landing gear, the boat and everything. We glided in smoothly and there wasn't one scratch on that boat. That was when I got the reputation of being "able to land on a dime".

On another occasion, the same company loaded a roll of about eighteen hundred pounds of steel cable into my Otter. The door was removed and the cable loaded with a front-end-loader. It was then strapped securely to the floor in a rolling position. Two men came along, attached with ropes tied to the back of my seat. Their job was to untie the straps and roll the cable to the door. I would then roll the aircraft and drop the cable at a precise location near the creek-bed. As I arrived at the drop-run, I lowered the flaps halfway, and the men rolled the cable back and through the door.

After searching for the cable for two days, the prospecting outfit found their cargo, exactly where they had asked me to drop it. They just couldn't believe a drop could be so precise. They could have saved two days of searching, if only they'd had more faith in my ability as a pilot.

It was about midnight one time in 1966 when a *Grand Duc Mining Company* boss came, woke me up and asked me to fly in to the mining-camp about twenty-five miles northeast of Stewart, to pick up a fellow who had suffered a heart attack. I said I'd give it a try. Of course it was very dark and would be darker still in the mountains. I asked them to put a truck at each end of the runway with lights on, so I could clearly see where to land. Well, I climbed up and went through the pass of the Scotty Dogs.

The runway was just a little over 1,000 feet long. I overshot the runway the first time, then went back and took another run at her. The second time I made it. However the patient died, so I had gone in for nothing. Bill Ross got smudge pots on the runway and I returned home that same night.

PART THREE

LUCK RUNS OUT

Grand Duc Slide

CLOSE CALLS AND MISHAPS

Sometimes landings could be very rough. I remember the time the spreader bar between the floats broke on the river. I had run out of open water and had to turn a blind corner. Luckily there was a gradual bank and I was able to make repairs right there.

Another close call of a different nature was when I was grounded at Leduc because of bad weather. I'd had a gnawing feeling in my gut and just had to get out of there. Finally, just before dark, there was a clearing and I flew out. Bill Ross lit the runway in Stewart so I could land in the dark. The next morning 22 to 27 people were killed in the big slide at the Grand Duc mining camp.

One time, I was coming out of Tide Lake, near Stewart, when I ran into a snowstorm. I flew around the mountain and the weather just followed me faster. I couldn't see where I was going, but I caught a glimpse of a small lake and decided to make a try for it. I pulled the throttle back and put the flaps down. I told Les, a mechanic from the *Caterpillar Tractor Company*, to "hold on tight; it's a small lake and I just hope we hit it."

Well, we landed and the plane came to a stop. However, we broke through the ice and the prop started hitting water. We took the tools out of the aircraft and, later, a helicopter came to pick us up. The water was only one-and-a-half feet deep. Bill Ross, my aviation engineer, and Bill Rayson the R.C.M.P. officer for Stewart, went up and turned the aeroplane around and raised it onto dry land.

Two days later the ice had got to four inches thick. Had we left the plane up there when it was getting colder, we'd never have gotten her out. I got back into the aircraft, warmed up the engine, put the flap down and took off, literally - on thin ice.

One afternoon I was coming in very late and looking for a landing strip, which was marked out close to a big waterhole in the ice. Flying into the wind, I touched the rough ice and broke the landing gear. It took about a week to make the necessary repairs and then they had to fly in another propeller. That was a cold time. On occasions like that, I often had to stay with the plane to keep it from freezing solid by removing and heating the engine oil and removing ice buildup from the fuselage. I'd be at it day and night with only brief periods of sleep.

On February 14, 1948, I was flying Art van Summers and a load of furs into Summit Lake, about forty miles north of Prince George. The engine stopped when we were just south of the lake. Due to strong head winds, I was unable to make a clearing and ended up going into the trees. We had about a million dollars worth of furs on board when the aeroplane broke in half. Luckily there was no fire and we did manage to salvage all the furs, although the plane was in very bad shape to say the least.

Another time, on Shaft Creek, south of Telegraph Creek, we had stopped for lunch. I had three or four miners with me, and a cook. After lunch, we got set to take off and the battery was dead, and so I wrapped rope around the hub to pull-start the engine. The prop took the rope and slapped my hat and glasses off. I never did find those glasses. We flew back to Stewart. Luckily, I still had my head.

Sometimes, when there was time, I would take the fellows for an hour or so of fishing. Then there were private fishing parties for the mining company. We caught mainly Arctic Char and lake trout.

On one trip, a fellow got a fishhook in his hand. The doctor was along. He asked me for a pair of metal cutters from my toolbox and cut the hook and pulled it out easily.

I brought some government fellows into Nahanni, in the North West Territories. Landing and takeoff were in a very tight space and we had to push out into the water before starting the engine. This time we were out in the water, just a short distance above the Virginia Falls - 316 feet high. The engine wouldn't start. The engineer was supposed to hold the plane but he had let go and jumped on for some reason.

We were getting nearer and nearer to the cataract and just about ready to jump from the plane. At the last minute the engine "took a hook". *This is a pilot's term for caught or started.* As we became airborne, I was barely able to avoid the big rock in the centre of the falls. That was a close call!

Once, around 1956, I was forced down in the North West Territories with a bad engine that couldn't be fixed. The game warden was running predator control for the caribou, which were being wiped out by wolves. He and I had to spend a few days in a tent while a new engine was rounded up. It was sixty-two below, and finally we had installed a brand new engine. As always in cold weather, I had drained the oil and kept it warm.

At night we would cover the engine with a tent and light a glow pot. When it was that cold, the gas would jell and we couldn't fly. Even at forty-five below we stayed put. We would wake up in the mornings and find the snow packed down by wolves, yet we had heard nothing and there was not a wolf in sight. When it finally got warm enough, we heated up the oil and had to drain her and start again several times.

We were finally able to start the new engine and, with some sputters and gasps, we got that icebox up into the air.

On one occasion when I was flying a Junkers 34, the fuel pump gave out. There was nowhere for a smooth landing so I went down in the trees. The plane split in two but all I got was a twisted ankle. I guess I'd always been lucky. By the way, they got the plane out of the bush and put her back together and she flew again.

LUCK RUNS OUT

There came the time I was not to be quite so lucky. On October 14, l968, I was just finishing a contract with *Grand Duc Mine* at Leduc. They had a short strip, a little over one thousand feet, at the foot of Leduc Mountain. Downdraughts, updraughts and crosswinds made landing and take off from that site quite difficult at times.

Bill Ross, my engineer, had a bad feeling as I prepared to take off with six barrels of high- test gas that had been pre-loaded. As I remember now, I sensed I had also lost my own bravado. Somehow, a feeling of impending doom was hard to shake.

This was to be my second trip of the day and bad weather was coming in fast. This wasn't even to be my own plane but another Otter that was loaded and ready to go.

I should have paid attention to my premonition, but instead, I shook the feeling off. I had been in dangerous situations so many times before. After all, if anyone was to get the job done, I was always ready to fly.

I got up over the Frank Mackey Glacier when I knew I'd have to turn back. Fresh snow on the glacier can be like glassy water and with an overcast sky it can be very difficult to tell how high one is flying. I decided to go around by what is known as the "Five Thousand Foot Pass". Although the clouds were coming down, I was able to see quite clearly through the Pass and I could see the floor of the valley below. I dropped down from 5500 feet until I was nearer to the valley floor. Then when I turned up the Leduc River, I got hemmed in.

I was making circles at 4500 feet trying to find a clearing but was trapped. It was my intent to climb to nine thousand feet and make an 180 degree turn back to Stewart. A very strong wind came up the narrow valley. I tried making it down to the creek, but a sudden gust blew me into vertical rock.

The right wing of the Otter hit the corner of the cliff, causing the nose of the aircraft to swing into the bluff, knocking off the nose-section with the engine. The plane fell thirty feet until she hit a small tree, which held my fuselage to the rock wall. I was knocked unconscious.

When I came to, I found myself still strapped to my seat, lying against the pilot's cabin door as the fuselage was lying partly on its side. I knew there was something wrong with my face but I also noticed two small fires just below me.

I could not get out through the cabin door, so I made my way cautiously through the fuselage. There I found two barrels of helicopter gas. The other barrels had gone out through the wall of the plane as if the side of the Otter had been opened with a giant can opener.

Realizing the aircraft was on fire, I rolled the drums of high test out, and watched them drop two hundred to three hundred feet. I knew I would rather risk falling than going up in one gigantic explosion.

I looked around for my sleeping-robe, but it was gone. Then I realized my robe and emergency ration-kit were back in my own plane. With my shoe and pant-leg on fire, I jumped, landing in about one-and-a-half feet of snow.

As I began sliding down the face of the mountain, I grabbed out at some branches and managed to stop my fall. Then I saw I was on a small ledge but I knew the plane's gas tanks would blow up at any moment. I crawled along the ledge as far from the plane as I could.

The snow had put out the fire on my shoe and pant-leg. I waited for what seemed an eternity for the tanks to blow. Then they exploded, one-by-one. The plane shook so violently, I thought it was going to fall on me and carry me down the mountain side.

After the explosions, it took me more than half-an-hour on that narrow ledge to get back under the tail of the aircraft.

I had hit the mountain at 12.20 p.m. but was not sighted until 2.30 p.m., although a 240 B helicopter had flown over the site twice. A small helicopter sighted the wreckage, but the pilot sent out the message that there were no survivors.

The Principal of a school in Stewart, who was helping in the search, had seen me move under the tail of the plane. He had a hard time convincing the search party that he had really seen anyone alive. However, he insisted on a second look and they came back.

When they saw me, they dropped a heavy parka. Then they landed the search helicopter at the top of the mountain above me and tried to get to me. As it was getting dark they were unable to reach me that night, so they returned to the foot of the mountain.

Trying to stop the bleeding on my face, I realized the whole side was wide-open. I was on that tiny ledge and did not dare move any more for fear I would pass out and fall into the abyss below.

Feeling ill and dizzy and fighting off the pounding pain, which gripped my whole body, I somehow managed to remain reasonably alert. I knew my life depended on my remaining conscious. I thought of Jean and the kids. Memories of so many happy times helped keep me awake. Sometimes I imagined hands reaching for me. I guess I must have been delirious. That was the longest night of my life.

The next morning, they flew back, to see if I was still alive. I heard the sound of the helicopter and made some kind of wave with one arm. Then they dropped me off a thermos of coffee, a chocolate bar, and a note stating they were going to cut the top out of a drum and lower it to me on a rope to lift me out.

While they were gone, the big helicopter came back with a climber's belt at the end of a nylon rope. Somehow I managed to crawl into the belt and when I gave the signal, they gently lifted me up. Then they lowered me to the valley below.

I remember looking up as we descended. The helicopter was dropping faster than I was and I began to worry that the rope holding me would get tangled in the tail rotor-blades. Miraculously we made it to the valley floor below where several men and a doctor were waiting for me and put me on a blanket. They had to pry my hand from the rope, I was hanging on so tightly.

I passed-out. From then on I wavered in and out of consciousness. I had lost a lot of blood. They took me out at 9 a.m. and at 3 p.m. I came to on intravenous.

The rescue team flew me first to the hospital in Stewart. Propped up in the helicopter, I overheard the pilot talking to the doctor. He was remarking that the weather looked too bad to proceed to Stewart. I heard the doctor say that since I had lost so much blood, he was doubtful I'd even make it to Stewart. I was conscious enough to suggest that below the cloud in the valley, the way would be clear and they could follow the river to Stewart. Then I passed out.

When we landed, I regained consciousness and wanted to walk into the nursing station. They carried me in on the blanket. In the room, the nurses started to undress me. I said, "Oh, no you're not. Get out!" They sent in Bill Ross, my engineer friend and he got me started and then I passed out again.

I've since heard that the nurses had the door partly open and watched the whole procedure but I don't remember any of that.

At three in the afternoon, I was transported to the airport, where I was loaded into a twin-engine Grumman Goose. I remember arguing with the ambulance crew to load me on feet-first not headfirst and I heard Bill Ross explain "That miserable old beggar will still be giving orders even after he's dead."

In Prince Rupert they sent me up to the operating room but all they could do was bandage me up. At two in the morning, the doctor came to inform me that I would have to sit up for the trip to Vancouver, to avoid any further loss of blood.

Lying in the Vancouver General Hospital Emergency ward, I felt cold. A drunk was hitting one of the nurses so I tried to get up but my legs wouldn't carry me. Then I told the nurse to hit him back.

I remained in the Vancouver General for several weeks while plastic surgeons worked on my face.

* * * * *

People have asked me what I would change if I had my life to live over again. I don't think I'd change a moment of it. I don't think there can be any experience more rewarding and beautiful than flying free with the eagles.

I will always be able to picture those beautiful sunsets where the air was clean and where people never had to lock their doors. Although I have lost my eyesight, I can still see the Aurora Borealis shimmering in the long night. One of the most awesome spectacles I have witnessed in the Arctic was the "Purple Dawn", when the first light refracted through ice crystals and turned everything to a glorious purple.

Those memories can never be taken from me.

EPILOGUE

After more than thirty-five years of flying all over British Columbia and Alberta, with much time spent along the Arctic Coast, in the Yukon, in Alaska and in the Northwest Territories, Pat Carey retired from flying on that October l4, 1968. Pat's eyesight failed soon after the crash, a result of head and facial injuries. His only regret was that he'd never be able to pilot a plane again although he was, on occasion, invited to accompany some of those he'd gotten to know so well over the years.

Pat and his wife moved to the Sunshine Coast before the year was up. Pat bought a mobile home and, with his son, cleared some bush and built a pad. The two lived happily in Sechelt for many years.

Following a life in which he had been able to achieve more than most men or women can even dream of, Pat Carey passed from this world on October 9th, 1999, having just celebrated his 96th birthday.

The Indian Chief up there came into the general store where I was getting some supplies. He said: "I'm going to name you 'White Eagle', you're always flying and always helping people out."

Rutherford Press

www.ingramcontent.com/pod-product-compliance
Lightning Source LLC
Chambersburg PA
CBHW072012040426

42447CB00009B/1604